PEARL BEYOND PRICE

Pearl beyond Price
The Attractive Jesus

David Day

Fount
An Imprint of HarperCollins*Publishers*

Zondervan
P.O. Box 749, Harrow HA1 1DP, UK
Grand Rapids, Michigan 49530, USA

First published in Great Britain and the USA in 2001
by Zondervan

1 3 5 7 9 10 8 6 4 2

A catalogue record for this book is available
from the British Library

ISBN 0 00 711568 7

Printed and bound in Great Britain by
Creative Print and Design (Wales), Ebbw Vale

For Rosemary

Contents

PREFACE

Books about Jesus must run into thousands by now and the reader may wonder how I dare offer another one. The brief answer is that I was unable to refuse the gracious invitation of James Catford of HarperCollins on behalf of the Archbishop of Canterbury. Now, with the undertaking completed, I gladly take this opportunity of thanking him for his encouragement and patience.

The longer answer is that in recent years I have become convinced that if Christians could only rediscover the sheer attractiveness of Christ, it would be the key to a reinvigorated discipleship, a more authentic church life and a more engaging style of evangelism. Like most Christians I go through periods of frustration at ecclesiastical trivial pursuits, despondency at church attendance statistics and irritation at my own spasmodic commitment. Furthermore, I suspect that many who will not go near a church would find Christ as magnetic a figure as the crowds around the sea of Galilee did, if only he were less diligently hidden by his followers. I believe that the answer to all these problems is for us to find again that one pearl beyond price.

In 1909 George Tyrrell criticized von Harnack's attempt to reconstruct the historical Jesus as 'only the reflection of a liberal Protestant face, seen at the bottom of a deep well'. These words haunt everyone who tries to produce a portrait of Christ. I am resigned to the fact that I will inadvertently have disclosed a great deal about myself in this book. What makes Jesus attractive to me is necessarily personal. But I also hope that the resulting picture is recognizably the Jesus of the gospels.

The book is personal but that does not mean that I have written it without assistance. I would like to thank those groups and congregations that heard early drafts in the form of addresses and sermons and particularly the congregation at St Nicholas, Durham. A great company of friends were cajoled or inveigled into reading chapters and I am happy to inscribe their names on the roll of martyrs: John Pritchard, Kate and Colin Macpherson, Gavin and Fran Wakefield, David Wilkinson, Dale Hanson, Alison Moore, Peter and Ann West. My children commented on much of the book and will be pleased to know that they can now stop avoiding me. And my thirteen-year-old grand-daughter, Emma, rose from her sick bed, all unbribed, to give me her views on two chapters. I am grateful to them all.

A special word of thanks must go to Colin Patterson for his creative comments about questions for reflection and discussion. I did not always take his advice and now regret not including his suggestion for a follow-up exercise – 'this week try kissing some frogs and see what princesses you can find'. My good friend Walter Moberly read the whole book with his characteristic thoroughness. His eagle eye spotted heresies, errors and infelicities of style; any that remain are the result of my stubbornness.

Finally, I would like to thank my wife Rosemary, who for the past nine months has done all my living for me. As an act of pure grace she also read the whole book, not once but many times in different versions. Towards the end she began to refer to me as 'that creature of the dark emerging from its hole'. In the circumstances I do not feel I can begrudge her such pleasantries.

FOREWORD BY THE
ARCHBISHOP OF CANTERBURY

I am delighted for several reasons that David Day accepted my invitation to write the Archbishop of Canterbury's Lent Book for 2002. The first is, unashamedly, because he is a special friend and the father-in-law of my eldest daughter! Of course, that is hardly a reason to invite someone to write a Lent book! The second reason is of course the one that matters – he is a superb communicator, a well-known author and a distinguished educationalist.

Why are Christians Christians? That apparently simple question lies behind every page of this exuberant Lent book, a book that almost bypasses Lent altogether in its joy and enthusiasm for the 'pearl beyond price'. Why are Christians Christians? David's answer is that it can only be because we are captivated by the attractiveness of Jesus Christ. 'Without an attractive Christ,' he asks, 'why believe at all?'

In the Book of Revelation, Jesus says to the Church in Ephesus, 'Endurance you have; you have borne up in my cause and have never become weary. However, I have this against you: the love you felt at first you have now lost' (Revelation 2:3–4). David's book is a sustained call for contemporary Christians to move beyond endurance back into love – the love that brought us to Christ in the first place. Again, he asks, 'Can we recapture the simple excitement which breathes through the pages of the New Testament?'

As David guides us through the gospels, however, it becomes clear that this 'simple excitement' is never *simplistic*. And while joy and enthusiasm are at the heart of his vision, the darkness of Lent is not forgotten. His book contains some challenging and indeed controversial reflections on evil and suffering and God's way with the world: reflections that remind us that the life of joyful faith and the life of rigorous thinking should not be separated. There is nothing safe or sentimental in these pages – but then there is nothing safe or sentimental in Jesus either. As C. S. Lewis said of Aslan, he's not a tame lion!

What I appreciate most about this book is the fresh and natural way David communicates Christian convictions. At the risk of being misunderstood, let me say straightforwardly that this is not a *pious* book – if by pious we mean mouthing empty platitudes of complacent conventional religion. It is instead a book that presents in fresh language the often unsettling truths of the Christian faith and does so in an intelligible and accessible manner. It is the kind of book that lends itself perfectly to group discussion as well as private study. So it is with great enthusiasm that I commend David's book. May you and I find Jesus Christ a 'pearl beyond price'.

+ George Cantuar

Archbishop of Canterbury

CHAPTER I

A PEARL BEYOND PRICE?

Some years ago I was helping to take a mission in a neighbouring church serving a large housing estate. Each evening, meetings were held in the homes of church members, to which neighbours were invited. At one of these meetings we sat and listened to the story of a young man who had recently come to faith. I remember the natural and unchurchy way he described his experience. He had not yet learned to talk like a Christian and what he said was completely free of jargon. In the middle of his talk he suddenly said, 'The thing is, Jesus Christ really *motivates* me.'

It is difficult for me to communicate the effect of that remark, tossed out in a broad Geordie accent. He might have been speaking about a football coach. I caught a glimpse of the sheer attractiveness, the pulling power, of the living Christ. Christianity for him had not yet become a routine, a creed or a code of conduct. He had been captivated by the person of Jesus. Like the man in the parable, he had found a pearl of great value and had sold up everything in order to get it. Ten years later I hear that he is a pillar of his local church. I hope he's not lost that first vision of Christ that drew him into faith.

In the gospels few people met Jesus without being affected in some way. It is the same today. A young woman went to church one Sunday and heard a sermon on Jesus' radical teaching about money. The words 'You cannot serve God and Money' came to her as clearly as if Christ were speaking directly. On an impulse she tipped the contents of her purse into the offering plate. It was an act of devotion and she felt liberated after it – even though she and her husband discovered they had no money for the ticket machine in the car park.

An international student studying in this country was befriended by a fellow-student who was a Christian. Later she became a Christian herself. As she reflected on what had happened to her she said of her fellow-student, 'She built a bridge of friendship into my heart and over the bridge walked Jesus.'

A student in Edinburgh was given a book about Jesus by a friend. Having nothing better to do, he started to read it one Saturday morning and found that he was unable to put it down. He finished the whole book by the late afternoon. At that point he had the strange feeling that this Jesus was present in the room. He knelt down and handed over the control of his life to the person who had stepped out of the pages of the book.

THE ATTRACTIVE CHRIST

Jesus is the heart of the Christian faith. Even in a culture that has given up on the church, the person of Jesus still commands respect. In this book I want to look at familiar stories in the hope that he will once more surprise us with the relevance of his teaching and the power of his presence. The portrait the gospels give us is an attractive one and it reminds us that Christianity is unashamedly centred on Christ. Jesus is the beginning of faith, the embodiment of the good news and the master we are called to obey. He is the path and the prize, the way, the truth and the life.

It may seem strange to speak of the 'attractiveness' of Christ. Hidden in the word 'attractive' is the Latin verb *traho* – to draw or pull. It is familiar to us through a line in the Christmas carol, *In Dulci Jubilo*: *Trahe me post te* – draw me after you. In Christ the pulling power of God is seen at its clearest. Jesus was a magnetic personality. His teaching drew large crowds. John's gospel sets out his astounding claim, 'If I am lifted up, I will draw all people to me.' Peter told Jesus early on in his Galilean ministry, 'Everyone is looking for you.' Almost every episode in the gospels puts Jesus at the centre. All eyes are upon him.

We can see something of this in the way Mark concludes his account of Jesus and the leper (Mark 1:40–45). Towards the end of the story Jesus tells the leper not to speak about his healing; the man's response is to spread the news abroad. I have heard a number of sermons that have pointed out how the man's wilfulness upset Jesus' plans: 'He was no longer able openly to enter a town.' 'In like manner,' preachers warn us, 'we, if we are not obedient, may spoil what God intends to do.'

But there is an alternative way of reading Mark's purpose. What if he wants to describe a man who has had his life turned inside out? What if he wants to say, 'Once this Christ has touched your life, you cannot stay silent'? Then we understand that the man has got to talk. The words pour out uncontrollably. We can imagine his thoughts: 'I know he said, "Tell no one; just go to the priest and show yourself, offer appropriate offerings for cleansing ..." But how can I keep silent? I was dead and am alive. I was rejected and now I am restored. I was filthy and now I am clean. And shall I not speak? If I were silent the very stones would shout.' So Mark ends the story with a snapshot. Jesus can no longer enter a town openly. He is forced to keep to the lonely places, far from the centres of population, and has to wander in the hills of golden Galilee. Then Mark presses the point home – Jesus cannot be hidden: *'They came to him from everywhere.'*

IN AND OUT OF THE PAGES

It may save misunderstandings if at the outset I say something about the way I want to approach the theme. Most of the book will focus on the portrait of Jesus the gospels give us, though I have felt free occasionally to stray into other parts of the New Testament. I am aware of the vast amount of scholarship that has been devoted to digging beneath the surface of the text of the gospels in order to uncover 'the real Jesus'. I too am interested in the quest for the historical Jesus and its results, and am impressed by the sustained disciplined inquiry it represents.

But if we wish to encounter the living Christ, I believe we shall do better to turn to the portraits we have received. Since the time of the early church, Christians have found Christ in the scriptures. I am not sure how much is to be gained for our purposes by trying to get behind these portrayals to some more authentic or primitive picture. Andrew Louth presses this point even further and makes it a matter of trust: 'We become Christians by becoming members of the Church, by *trusting* our forefathers in the faith. If we cannot trust the Church to have understood Jesus then we have lost Jesus: and the resources of modern scholarship will not help us to find him.'[1]

The four gospels are the record of Jesus as he was remembered by those who knew him, loved him and wished to follow him faithfully. It is the experience of the church that the living Christ is encountered in these documents. We need to live in the world of the story and trust that he will meet us there, and also that, in a mysterious way, he will meet us in our own world at the same time.

This confidence in the Christ who meets us in the pages accounts for a certain lack of consistent practice on my part. On the whole, the gospels refer to 'Jesus' and the rest of the New Testament to 'Christ'. It used to be common to read of the 'Jesus of History' and the 'Christ of faith'. I have made no attempt to be scrupulous about the use of Jesus and Christ; the reader will find that the names are used more or less interchangeably. I hope this will not be taken as evidence of an untidy mind. It reflects my conviction that the Jesus whom we meet in the gospels is the Christ who joins us, walks with us on the road, opens the scriptures and makes himself known in the breaking of bread.

One further point. I do not want it to seem that God appears in this book as if by accident. Christ is its focus and its theme. But any thought that God is to be found only in the shadows, clearing his throat diffidently and apologizing for muscling in

---

1 Andrew Louth, *Discerning the Mystery*, Oxford: Clarendon Press, 1983, p. 93.

on our conversation with Jesus misconstrues my intention. Without revisiting the finer points of Nicaea or Chalcedon I still want to affirm that Jesus is God incarnate. In other words, the character, activity and purpose of God can be 'read off' from what we see in Jesus. God is like Christ. Christ embodies the fullness of God the Father, just as the Spirit of God brings his presence personally into our lives. In finding Jesus we find the Father and the Spirit. We set out to rediscover the attractive Christ but, as we do, we bear in mind his words: 'If anyone loves me, he will obey my teaching. My Father will love him, and we will come to him and make our home with him' (John 14:23).

The Baggage we Bring to the Book

As we prepare to encounter Jesus through some very familiar stories we are aware that none of us travels light. Christians of the twenty-first century bring to the quest their own experiences, expectations, hopes and anxieties. Some of these we share with each other, they are the product of our time and culture. Some are particular to ourselves. We cannot pretend that they don't exist, but when we face up to them we find that they ask us searching questions. The rest of this chapter will explore some of these concerns. Do you recognize yourself in any of them? Has the attractive Jesus anything to say about them? My hope is that as we rediscover him, we shall hear him speak to each of us his liberating word.

Going through the Motions of Discipleship

I begin with the grimly realistic. For many the Christian life is most accurately described as 'dutiful observance'. They hear exhortations about 'moving from maintenance to mission', but are disinclined to leap up with enthusiasm. Of course, no one can deny that there is some merit in doggedly keeping on keeping on, but routine and habit deaden the spirit. A faith that consists of nothing but tight-lipped resolution can hardly be described as life-enhancing.

In such a mood, worship becomes dutiful, no more than going through the motions and waiting for the Final Blessing to signal the moment when they can go home. 'Lord,' they say thankfully, 'at last you give your servant his discharge in peace.' It is disturbing to find that many who attend church regularly confess to feeling worse after the service than before. Prayer becomes a burden, vain repetitions of yesterday's shopping list. Giving becomes a prudent calculation of how much won't be missed. Service means fulfilling your slot in the flower rota or listening to old Mr Garratt's interminable reminiscences of the day he saved Britain from the barbarous hordes.

It is easy to stand at the edges of the gospel stories, a knowing smile playing around our lips. 'It isn't quite as straightforward as that,' we think, wishing it might be so. But following Christ normally brings joy, not a deadening routine. The question asked of us is: Can we recapture the simple excitement that breathes through the pages of the New Testament?

Burdened by the Spiritual Experience of the Saints

We come to stories we have heard many times before. As we read, it is almost impossible not to hear the saints murmuring in the background. Often this is language in overdrive – the words of the great hymns and liturgies of the church, the meditations of holy people and heroes of faith. What should inspire us can sometimes weigh us down. This is the burden of holy history. We feel the uncomfortable gap that opens up between their robust and vibrant grasp of devotion and our tentative fumblings.

For example, Bernard of Clairvaux, commenting on *The Song of Songs*, wrote, 'Jesus is honey in my mouth and a song of Jubilee in my heart.' The Cure d'Ars prayed, 'I love you, O my God, and I would rather die loving you than live not loving you.' The author of the spiritual classic, *The Cloud of Unknowing* exhorts us, 'And smite upon that thick cloud of unknowing with a sharp dart of longing love and go not thence for anything that befalleth.' Dame Julian says with confidence, 'I could with the help of our Lord and his grace, have increase of and be lifted up to more heavenly knowing and higher loving.'

We enter a different world when we go to the average church meeting. Recently a minister told me that he had spent what seemed like hours desperately trying to persuade a couple that the monthly car boot sale really was less important than worship. Many Christians are uncomfortable with the language of their holy predecessors when asked to speak about their faith. The great saints seem to dwell on another planet, breathing a different kind of air, or living on something that is probably a banned substance.

It is easy to mock, but perhaps the great saints just knew Christ more intimately than we do. Perhaps he was more real to them or they were more open about letting him into their ordinary lives. The language of hymns and liturgies, of prayers and meditations need not leave us amused or bemused. We would do better to take it as an invitation to search diligently for Christ. Gilbert of Hoyland says, 'Unroll the scroll of life, the scroll which Jesus himself unrolls or, rather, which is Jesus himself. Wrap yourself in him.' Can we enter more deeply into the portrait of Jesus in the scriptures that so intoxicated our fathers and mothers in the faith?

Embarrassed to Speak about Christ

Following Christ has always involved mission. Good news has to be passed on. The great commission to go into all the world lets no one off the hook. Throughout the ages of the church, each generation has rethought the good news in order to present the eternal message in new words for a changed world. But what is to be done when the news is no longer new and doesn't seem particularly good? And what is to be said to a world that has changed so drastically that it no longer has the equipment to pick up our signals?

An amusing article by A. A. Gill illustrates the problem that results. He is describing the experience of being interviewed by Lynn Barber for the *Observer*:

In passing, really without thinking, I mentioned that I was a Christian. Well, that did it. Lynn almost inhaled

her asparagus, her eyebrows shot off the top of her head. Nostrils bulging, she waved her arms as if for a passing lifeboat. 'A Christian!' she gasped, Lady Bracknell style, 'A Christian, as in believing in God, the God, that God?'
Oh dear. Yes, that God.
'No you're not, you can't possibly be.'

Later on he identifies the heart of the problem.

> It's not just that nobody svelte, stylish or savvy believes; it's that faith firmly puts you on the nerdy team, playing alongside fundamentalist loonies, hysterically joyous born-agains with mad hair, home-made jumpers and no sex life, bearded vicars on motorbikes, jam makers, angel spotters, cross burners, bead counters and the Archbishop of Canterbury. Sometimes the one thing that seems to unite every frothingly barmy simpleton on the planet is a belief in God, and I'm with them.[2]

Following Christ has never been easy. There was a time when it might have involved being torn apart by lions or being burned alive. Even today in some parts of the world discipleship speaks of beatings and fire-bombed churches. In Western Europe we have to acknowledge that the cross which the Christian shoulders is less painfully physical – the pressure takes a different form – but it is still a cross. Few of us live in fear of martyrdom; most of us know what it is to flinch at the question asked of Peter: 'Surely you are one of them?' But perhaps part of the answer is to rediscover the radical, life-loving, unshockable Jesus whom no one ever put on the nerdy team.

---

2 A. A. Gill, *Sunday Times*, 26 March 2000.

Ashamed of the Way the Church has Distorted the Face of Christ

In many quarters the church is a synonym for racism, child abuse, persecution of minority groups, greed, small-mindedness, prudery, snobbery and elitism. Its record is not good – history places it fairly consistently on the side of the masters, the oppressors, the mine owners, the slave owners, the squire, the laird and the folk up at the Hall. Of course, this is a gross caricature, but those whose lives gloriously contradict the stereotype tend to be forgotten in the headlines about the next priest to be convicted for molestation or the next nun in court for beating orphanage children. 'Suffer the little children to come unto me' is bitterly ironical. For many people, Jesus is not an attractive figure simply because they cannot get near him.

The answer is not to deny the appalling record of institutional Christianity, though where Christians do shine like lights in the world it doesn't hurt to point this out. The ultimate answer is to catch a fresh vision of the man who went about doing good, who scandalized the complacent, cared about justice, stood up to the powerful, welcomed the poor, blessed little children and, in the end, held back nothing, not even his life.

Shaken by the Hostility of the World

Last year I joined an Internet chat group on Christian apologetics. I thought it would be interesting to listen to and join in informed debate about Christianity. I needn't have bothered. The contributions represented some of the most ill-informed and vitriolic outbursts I have ever read. The ferocity of the respondents ought to be the subject of special research. Their naked hostility made a profound impact on me. It invited some kind of explanation.

Why is the Christian faith so deeply repugnant to so many? What have the contributors experienced of Christians or the church that they feel the need to express such immoderate opinions, such loathing mingled with hysterical contempt?

It wasn't just that Christians were perceived as old-fashioned and strait-laced. It had more to do with a rage that anyone should have the impudence to try to impose on thinking people a belief system at once so ill founded, superstitious, corrupting and oppressive.

This attitude is not confined to those who log on to Internet chat groups. A letter to *The Times* fires a provocative salvo: 'Fortunately, most youngsters are learning to think for themselves and not follow the lemmings. Simply, they cannot accept something unproven, unverifiable and highly unlikely merely on the superstitious ramblings of ancient texts. Jesus preached many humanitarian values. Why not just accept them as that?'[3]

Brian Molko, lead singer with the band *Placebo*, reminisced about his Christian upbringing in these words: 'When your parents tell you that there's this fat guy with a beard in a red suit that comes down the chimney and gives you presents, you kind of believe it. And when your parents tell you that there's this thin guy with a beard who died on a cross for you, you kind of believe in it too. I find it interesting that people lie to you from day one.'[4]

'Faith firmly puts you on the nerdy team.' Faith means 'you follow the lemmings' and believe the lies people tell you 'from day one'. It would be a complex task to uncover the roots of such negative feelings. Certainly, for those who speak like this the attractive Christ has been well-disguised.

The cavalier reaction is to say that they are an evil and adulterous generation and Satan has them in his thrall. That may let off a little steam and make us feel better, but it will not do. It is more likely that those who feel angry have been the victims of overzealous dogmatism. The gospel does make breathtaking pronouncements. It is marked by affirmations that lay claim to the whole of life. Unfortunately, it is all too

---

3 Geoffrey Smith, letter to *The Times*, 5 July 2000, p. 23.
4 Mark Edwards, 'Rock', *Sunday Times*, 16 July 2000

easy to pass on the good news in a way that makes it sound like bad news, to hector, browbeat and condemn. In his time Jesus was a scandal and a stone of stumbling. He provoked anger and hostility. But there is a difference between the inevitable offence of the gospel and the offensiveness of its servants.

Perhaps many of those who are hostile have never encountered a portrait of Jesus that is responsibly drawn, faithful to the texts, and sensitively presented. We surely believe that such a portrait carries its own power to draw people to Christ. Like it or not, Christians are caught up in a public relations exercise on his behalf.

Convinced that our World Needs Christ

Not everyone is hostile to Christianity, far from it. The church I attend recently decided to call at all the houses in the immediate neighbourhood. The visitors made an encouraging discovery: those who answer the door are people very much like oneself. They are cautious – but these days that is a sensible policy when confronted with people on the doorstep. They are usually courteous and often interested, even pleased, to find that the local church has bothered to make contact. Many churches have developed a pattern of asking if there is anything the householder would like the church to pray for and have been amazed at the response. When the church does the kind of thing the church should do and offers support rather than asking for money then the results are surprisingly positive.

Jesus told his disciples that the fields were white for harvest. It sometimes needs an act of faith to see this but he tends to be right on such matters. Here are some snapshots, taken almost at random, from one church over a period of three months: A young couple turn up at church because of the birth of their first child and they 'just want to do the best for him'. A graphic designer surfs the net for a church that will help him make sense of religion, and travels nearly twenty miles to attend. Two friends go to a dinner at a local hotel in order to find out more about a course on the basics of

Christianity. A woman suddenly returns to church after an absence of twenty years, because 'it's time I rediscovered something to base my life on'. Someone else goes on holiday to Israel and is so impressed by the sense of Christ's presence at the Sea of Galilee that she begins attending worship at her parish church. A young professional woman starts coming because a friend recommended it – and bought her a Bible. It is just not the case that everyone is implacably opposed to the Christian faith. The fields are white to harvest.

Of course, there are problems to be faced. The church attendance figures make sobering reading however you interpret them. A decade of evangelism has not filled the pews. At least one generation seems to have been lost, if only temporarily. The claims the church makes for the life of faith – joy, peace, victory, fulfilment, reconciliation – are not always borne out by the life of faith as the church lives it. Religious belief counts as low-status knowledge, crushed by the imperialistic advance of scientific method and terminology. Alternative and more fashionable views of the universe compete with the Christian world-view. Tests for the reality of what one believes seem private and idiosyncratic. Problems surround the nature of human personality, the coherence of the idea of survival after death, and the meaning of a world that contains an excess of pain and suffering. Throw in Sunday trading and we have reason enough to take a deep breath.

And yet, 'When he [Jesus] saw the crowds he had compassion on them, because they were harassed and helpless, like sheep without a shepherd' (Matthew 9:36). Can we see those who live around us with the eyes of Christ? He sees the woman who opens the electricity bill worrying how on earth she will find the money to pay it. And he knows that she is harassed. He sees men who have just been made redundant and knows that they are helpless to do anything about it. He sees the youths who vandalize a telephone kiosk and knows that they are like sheep without a shepherd. We are surrounded by people who are worried sick as they wait for the results of hospital tests, who have forgotten how to talk to their children, who move through relationships in the forlorn hope that this one will be better than the last, who regret their mistakes, are guilty about the damage they have done to others, fear death, chase happiness, wonder what it's all about and, in some cases, are screaming inside. And then there are those who seem to have no antennae for the spiritual, who are not especially hostile, just bewildered at the thought that any of it should have any relevance to them at all. But all, since they are human, wanting to be loved more than anything else in the world.

What do we have to offer? We are not those who sail through life untouched, coping triumphantly with all it throws at us. Our prayer is *Kyrie eleison* – 'Lord, have mercy'. But we are those who were once far off and now have been brought home. Can we renew our vision of the Christ who loves the lost and, seeing him afresh, communicate that vision of love to those who need it?

Needing to Rediscover the Attractive Christ for our own Sake

In the final analysis, our search for the attractive Jesus is not driven primarily by the desire to commend him to those outside the church. If talking about Jesus is no more than whistling to keep our spirits up, then the sooner it is abandoned the better. If faith in Christ is just a set of inspiring pictures useful for cheering oneself up on a dark day, then let's trade them in for a better set. They have to be pictures of someone real. We understand the concept of virtual reality only too well. Living in a world of virtual reality is what geeks do, hunched over their computers, interminably killing life-threatening robots, giants, killer dragons and karate-chopping warriors from the planet Zog. The virtual life, however entertaining, will not serve us well in the real world. Jesus has to be more real than Lara Croft.

Although we know this to be so, yet the spiritual climate is not hospitable to Christian faith. We hear the question 'How do you know you're not making it up?' It is in the air we breathe and none of us sits so snugly behind the double glazing that we do not shiver at the icy blasts blowing on the other side of the window. In such chilly weather it is perilously easy to doubt what we once held fast. We cannot ignore those difficult questions that are put to the church by the world outside. The least we can do is to acknowledge the criticisms and recognize that the voices outside us find answering echoes in the voices inside our heads. In fact, the believer knows, often better than the unbeliever, that the voices muttering inside put the case against faith rather more knowledgeably and forcefully than anything most outsiders can come up with.

In these circumstances it is sensible to tackle the problem areas as well as we can manage, to read, discuss, argue, reflect and finally come to a position that we can defend without putting our brains to sleep. We want to have a reason for the hope within us. God is not glorified by our wish that the problems would just go away and *reasonable faith* is in itself part of an integrated spirituality.

A SOMEWHAT EMBARRASSED ENCOUNTER WITH DELIGHT

But important though it is to have good grounds for believing, yet the dynamic of the Christian life comes from a relationship with the living Christ. The great danger epitomized in the words to the church of Ephesus is that 'we lose our first love' (Revelation 2:4). When this happens, every aspect of life is affected – belief, prayer, behaviour, obedience, trust, worship, mission – including our intellectual grasp of the faith.

It then becomes a matter of urgency to return to that vision which first grasped us. For if there is nothing in Christ that acts like a magnet on us, then we may as well give up. Without an attractive Christ, we are at a loss to explain faith or recommend the gospel. How can we, since the gospel will hardly be good news? If the love of Christ does not grip us, we can only speak of faith in tones of regret and struggle on with a dogged but unintelligible persistence. If there is no quality in Christ that haunts us and draws us to him, then it is hard to see why we should choose to follow him. Without an attractive Christ, why believe at all?

However, at the start of the journey I do not want the voices of suspicion, whether inside or outside one's head, to decide the route to be followed. We set out to see again the face of Christ, to remember what it was that first drew us to him and to recapture or to renew that first delight in him. As we enter into the scriptures we listen for that personal word that touches us where we are. We cannot make this happen. Christ is the Lord of surprise. We cannot demand that grace captivate us. For that we have to rely on him. In the fourth gospel Jesus says, 'If I am lifted up, I will draw all people to myself.' We trust that when we catch a glimpse of Christ, we shall be drawn to him in a renewed loyalty, love and obedience. But we cannot predict how this will happen or how we shall react. That is what makes discipleship exciting. For myself, I love the beautifully understated words of William Countryman. He is discussing 'the humanly impossible moment' of recognizing God's goodness and mentions that some respond to this with a kind of mystical self-transcendence. This is not the norm, however. 'Most of the time', he continues, 'it takes the simpler form of a somewhat embarrassed encounter with delight that casts all of life in a new light.'[5] I'll settle for that.

REFLECTION

Which incidents in the gospels epitomize the attractive Jesus for you? If you had to choose an image of Christ to represent him to

---

5 L. William Countryman, *The Poetic Imagination: An Anglican Spiritual Tradition*, London, Darton, Longman and Todd, 1999, p. 124.

- a particular friend
- a teenager
- someone who is hostile or suspicious of Christianity

what would you choose?

You are asked to suggest an image of Christ for a stained glass window in your church. What do you propose? How would you support your choice?

Discussion

'Faith puts you on the nerdy team.' Is there a discrepancy between how people view Jesus and how they view Christians? If so, why do you think this is?

In your experience, are 'the fields white to harvest'? What stories can you tell of Christ active in the lives of your friends and acquaintances?

Exercise

Collect a number of contrasting pictures of Jesus. Discuss with a friend what attracts or repels you in each?

Prayer

A prayer of St Anselm:

> Lord Jesus Christ,
> Hope of my heart, strength of my soul,
> Help of my weakness,
> By your powerful kindness complete
> What in my powerless weakness I attempt.
> My life,
> The end to which I strive,

Although I have not yet attained to love you as I ought,
Still let my desire for you
Be as great as my love ought to be.[6]

---

6 Sister Benedicta Ward (ed. and tr.), *The Prayers and Meditations of Saint Anselm with the Proslogion*, London, Penguin Books, 1988, p. 93.

CHAPTER 2

THE FAITHFUL FRIEND

'Without a friend thou canst not live well,' said St Thomas à Kempis, and our society would be inclined to agree with him. The really successful human being has lots of friends, appears on everyone's *A List* for parties and spends the summer celebrating the joys of friendship at 'lively resorts' like Ayia Napa. The perfect set-up for the eighteen–thirty age range is portrayed in the long-running series *Friends*, where an admittedly ageing cast share life and their eyeshadow in unrestricted intimacy. Friendship is vital to the good life, at times more important than family, and certainly more influential than parents.

JESUS AS FRIEND

The idea of Jesus as friend is common in the New Testament, even though the word itself is less frequent than you might expect. It is a rich image that speaks directly to our world. We cry out for friends who will never let us down. The 'buddy film', the police drama where each partner in the duo covers for the other, even *Friends*, all point to the strong appeal of the loyal friend whom you can trust. At the same time, every television soap depicts false friends who betray you. Few characters appear to be able to keep confidences. Backbiting and gossip prevail. Hardly has a secret been shared when it is passed on with relish. 'Without a friend thou canst not live well,' but where is the real friend to be found? Behind the chat lines and the Internet groups, the hen parties and stag nights lies a longing for a faithful friend.

Jesus said to his followers, 'You are my friends.' People often talk about Christianity as a system of beliefs, or a code of ethics or a significant social institution or a repository of 'Christian values'. As I look at the Christian faith what strikes me most forcibly is that it offers *friendship with a person*. In Jesus we meet the faithful friend, whose commitment to us never wavers. This friendship is good even to death. John Ireland's beautiful hymn links it with Good Friday:

> This is my friend, my friend indeed,
> who at my need his life did spend.

THE CHARACTERISTICS OF FRIENDSHIP WITH JESUS

Human friendship is marked by activities like keeping in contact, sharing personal news, being loyal to one another and doing things together. Friendship with Christ ought to involve similar experiences. Can we flesh out the idea?

Dignity: Being a Friend of Royalty

We do not take the initiative where Christ is concerned. He chooses his friends; they do not choose him. We might paraphrase Jesus' words in John 15:16 as 'It is *I* who have chosen *you* (and not the other way round)' – the word for 'I' is emphatic. What we might term our journey into faith, turns out with hindsight to be Christ's pursuit of us. He calls and we respond. He has been at work long before we begin to answer.

This fact has profound personal implications. From time to time we may catch someone name-dropping – hinting at a friendship with the rich and famous, even a nodding acquaintance with royalty. But to be chosen by Christ to be his friend ranks even higher than cocktails with the Beckhams. It is a source of dignity, for no one could despise themselves once they knew that they had been befriended by the Lord of Glory. I recall the amazement of one man when it was pointed out that Christ *liked* him. He had grown used to the thought that Christ loved him; after all, that was his job! But to be *liked* –

despite those character traits which were not very likeable! It was like a revelation to him that Christ was prepared to put up with his irritating foibles, unpleasant habits and unwashed socks.

Security: Laying Bare your Secrets

Once I had reason to interview over seventy teenagers about their faith. I soon discovered that the most popular image of Jesus was that of 'available friend'. He was a kind of confidant at the end of the mobile phone. They wanted him on an open line at all times. Like Radio 1 or MTV he was in the background chattering away. Such teenagers often enjoyed rich relationships with Christ. He was the friend with whom they could share everything – anxieties about homework, tension with parents, romantic interludes with the opposite sex. In many respects such friendships were models of intimacy, openness and vitality. Nothing was censored and all desires laid out before Christ.

It is assumed that the good friend is one with whom you can share everything. Paul writes about the Christian's freedom of speech – the privilege of coming boldly into Christ's presence and confiding in him (Romans 5:2; 2 Corinthians 3:12,17). This privilege includes sharing hopes, fears, plans and longings. All the satisfaction of revealing one's innermost thoughts to the journal ('Dear diary ...') has its parallel in prayer that is simple, direct, and without pretence or concealment. Christ is instantly available and in his presence there is no need for awkwardness or a stifling politeness.

It is easy to say that, of course. It may be more difficult to put it into practice. It is not easy to face, let alone speak about, aspects of ourselves that make us ashamed. Memories come back that have the power years later to make us blush. It is a painful exercise slowly to rerun the film. Is there anything in our prayer lives that we are aware of as being tacitly censored? Any topic, memory or person to which our inbuilt censor denies access? We wriggle uneasily or try to justify ourselves or find devious ways of not owning our bad parts or, most commonly, flinch from the open wound. Sadly, what we cannot bring into Christ's presence remains unhealed.

Confession of sin means more than saying a few words. In the most complex cases a person may need professional help to gain access to those parts of the personality the hymn calls 'the very wounds which shame would hide'. But whether alone or with help, it is possible to know liberty, release and freedom. Then we discover that to be open in the presence of Jesus is total security. To be known through and through is to find a rock on which we can stand and a source of healing. In prayer we can be vulnerable and open, finding the capacity to face the dark side of ourselves in safety.

One of the most powerful stories in the gospels shows Jesus dealing with the darkness in Simon Peter (John 21:15–17). Peter's brash words about never disowning Jesus have resulted in the threefold denial – 'I do not know the man'. Thus the friend of three years is betrayed in a moment, at the point when he most needs Peter's support. After the resurrection Jesus meets his former friend by the lake. There begins a painful process of remaking both the friendship and Peter. In front of the others, Jesus presses Peter to say publicly what he had publicly denied. 'Do you love me?' 'Yes' comes the awkward answer. The question is asked again – and again, each time nearer the bone. Peter is grieved by the interrogation but is unable to escape. In the end he reaches the point where he can only lay bear his soul before Jesus: 'Lord, you know me through and through. You know my heart. You know, in my desperate, pathetic way and despite my failure, you know that I love you.' Jesus' work is done. Peter has touched the rock.

Honesty: Saying What you Really Feel

At times freedom of speech may take a different course and spill over into complaint. Personal pain may be so great that we may feel like accusing our friend of indifference or neglect. This experience is enormously significant for plotting the dimensions of friendship with Christ. We can grant that friendship implies openness and honesty, laying bare the secrets of the heart and praying with fervour; but how far can we go?

The Old Testament, especially the book of Psalms, would appear to sanction almost any language. Complaint, lament, accusation, bitterness, sarcasm, anger, argument seem to be an integral part of what it understands by friendship with God. In the New Testament the tone is less strident, though Paul describes intensity in prayer (2 Corinthians 12:8) and there is a hint of lament in the cry 'How long?' Most Christians would like to borrow from the Old Testament the freedom to complain bitterly about their own situation and at times to berate God for what appear to be broken promises, undeserved suffering and culpable inactivity. Real friendships, we might feel, should be strong enough to survive such confrontational language. Indeed, God might even want to encourage it. After all, Jesus' cry of dereliction is taken from Psalm 22. What are the implications for friendship with Christ? It is certain that he will not break if we shout at him. Nevertheless, with some hesitation, I want to ask if the nature of friendship with God changes between the testaments. The new element is the crucifixion. Despite the rich portrayal of the love of God in the Old Testament it still lacks the embodiment of that love which the cross provides. As we allow the picture of Christ crucified to enter our imaginations and shape our relationship, so the savagery and raw accusation of the Psalms is tempered. Somewhere St Francis writes, 'If I am to complain, let me complain to Christ on the cross.' After all, 'This is my friend, my friend indeed, who at my need his life did spend.' It is all right to go on feeling grief and sorrow of spirit, to want to cry out 'Why?' and 'How long?', to take the long journey into Godforsakenness. A friendship that has to watch its words, that does not allow us to give shape to fear, pain or desolation, is a poor thing. However, let us remember that we speak in the shadow of the cross and the figure who looks down on us shares our darkness.

Authority: Hearing the Truth about Yourself

Christ chooses us. He is a friend, certainly, but a friend who is also a Master and who defines friendship not only by his choice of us but also by our obedience. Unfortunately, Christians are always only half a step away from *Christus domesticus*. We foolishly act as if we are doing him the favour of believing in him and honouring him with our patronage. It would be useful to have Christ at our beck and call, shaped conveniently to our needs.

The television sitcom *The Vicar of Dibley* bought into this notion of the patronized Jesus. The Revd Geraldine Granger keeps a picture of Christ on the wall and chats away to it (him). He is good to talk to, a little like her simple verger. But when she is about to enter upon a dubious relationship (with an actor last seen playing the part of a consultant in *Casualty*), she turns the portrait to the wall with the words 'Not your kind of evening'. This is one friend with a mind of his own, however. He is no pushover. Friendship carries obligations. Jesus said, 'You are my friends if you do what I command' (John 15:14).

An image of the authority of Jesus comes from a surprising source. In the letter to the church at Laodicea (Revelation 3:14–21) Jesus is pictured as standing at the door knocking. The passage is the source for the famous Holman Hunt painting of *The Light of the World* and is often taken to typify the gracious invitation of the gospel.

But in its context, Jesus at the door is a profoundly disturbing image. The little church at Laodicea probably didn't have much of a liturgy but even they would have believed that at their love feasts Christ was present at the meal. The letter contradicts that assumption: Christ is on the doorstep, wondering if you will let him in. It provokes the question 'What is he doing on the outside? And how did he get there?' Imagine the first-century equivalent of the eucharistic prayer 'The Lord is here'. And imagine the terrible response 'No, he isn't. He's outside.' How *can* he be outside?

I would like to know how Christ got there. At this point my imagination runs riot: Perhaps it went something like this: we had a sherry reception and he slipped away during the proceedings. No one saw him go but he felt out of place. Not really his scene. Quite a lot of his friends had not been invited. He thought, 'You don't need me here. You're OK on your own.' We looked around and he wasn't there.

Or – we deliberately showed him the door. We said, 'Sorry, you're spoiling the party. We don't feel that we can be as free as we would like to be. We relax a bit more if you're not here. Like watching television with a disapproving grandparent.'

Or – we moved to a new house and never invited him to the housewarming. We used to be inseparable. Couldn't have imagined an evening when he wouldn't have been first on the list. But we drifted – the way you do. Just a card at Christmas and Easter. And when we moved, we made the break.

Excuse my whimsical speculations. 'The Lord is here.' No, he isn't. He's outside knocking on the door. We're left with a picture of a party, all lights and noise inside and a figure on the doorstep, just out of range of the security light.

The letter to Laodicea describes Christ as The Amen, the faithful witness. The gift this faithful Lord gives me is the truth. He says quietly, 'This is the way it is between us.' I say to him, 'Exaggerating a bit, aren't we? I am rich, well-clothed and keen-eyed.' He says, 'You don't know you are destitute, naked and blind.'

The words continue, 'Somewhere you lost it. In church, you maintain the services, keep the plant going but have ceased to do justice. The zeal for evangelism cooled off. Your friends became people like you – all members of a congenial club. Private prayer was cut back to a few perfunctory minutes and then stopped. Worship became a formality. To meet the unreflective, naïve, wholehearted young Christian on fire for Christ became an embarrassment. You smiled at the lack of sophistication of the African church even as they healed the sick, walked on water and raised the dead. You learned to nuance and qualify everything. Now you are dying of good taste. I'd sooner you were a hardened atheist. I could get nearer to you. Habit, form, routine, stock responses – something has been cauterized.'

These are the words of The Amen, the faithful witness. Even so, 'Those whom I care for, I rebuke and shape with discipline – *those whom I care for.*' Faithful are the wounds of a friend. This is my friend and he speaks the truth.

Intimacy: Understanding his Mind

The key text is found in John 15:12–17. In the upper room Jesus says to the disciples, 'I no longer call you servants, because a servant does not know his master's business. Instead, I have called you friends, for *everything that I learned from my Father I have made known to you*' (15:15). The prime distinction is that between friend and slave (a more literal translation than 'servant'). A slave does not know what the master is doing. He is not privy to his plans. The friend, on the other hand, has access to the master's mind. The master shares his plans, intentions and outlook.

If this is so, why do we find it so difficult to see what's really going on in the details of our lives? The friend is supposed to know all that the master is doing, but discernment remains a tricky business. Am I to go for this job? Why does my illness continue? Should I marry this person? If I write this letter will it make matters better or worse? Shall we pour money into reordering the church? Why are my friends having such a bad time? The master is supposed to be sharing his plans, intentions and outlook. Do the words of Jesus apply to contemporary life?

It is the testimony of Christians down the ages that from time to time they do receive a specific word addressed to them – a word that comes to pass. In general, though, the sense of Jesus' words is that Christians have insight into the ways of God. Jesus shares with the disciples the knowledge of the kind of God God is, and, if we can put it this way, his preferred way of doing things, his 'house style'. The present and future may be obscure but the interpretative *key* is available to any Christian. Jesus shares with us his knowledge of a God who is love, who works out his purposes in the pattern of cross and resurrection, whose power is made perfect in weakness, whose wisdom often looks like folly from the perspective of the world and who, most importantly of all, may be trusted in the business of life. We may want more but it is enough.

It is easy to state this in a way that sounds arrogant, and it is not a licence to become more and more dogmatic about the future, nor to give daily updates on the activity of God as if he regularly consulted us about his diary. I once heard one of the leaders of the modern charismatic movement speak of 'a lady to whom the Deity gave so many messages that it was a wonder he had any time left to run the universe.' On the other hand, we must not disparage the amazing promise Christ gives. Christians do have insight into the private life of the universe; they do discern something of God's way with the world. And they do so because friendship with Christ includes a revelation of God's character and love.

Through this revelation Christ invites us to enter more deeply into the work of God in the world. He wants us to see more clearly how his grace is active in the most unlikely places, to understand how power is made perfect in weakness, to love with his love and to pray in ways that are in harmony with his will. 'I call you my friends' is both humbling and exhilarating. We make decisions responsibly and with prayer. Then we trust him to guide us. The astonishing, almost unbelievable fact, is that we are called by Christ to be co-workers with him in his world.

Activity: Caring for his Friends

Friendship with Jesus is not just a matter of 'tea for two, just Jesus and you'. We are expected to get involved with other people. The chief way of obeying the command of the Master is to love other Christians. Jesus said, 'My command is this: Love each other as I have loved you' (John 15:12). This is one of the signs that the friendship is alive.

Joan's story shows this principle at work. Joan is in her forties. She's pleasant, well dressed and has been going to St Barnabas for about ten years. She came to faith through an Alpha group; her husband, alas, thinks she is mad. She loves the worship at St Barnabas. She luxuriates in the songs and choruses. They're like a sauna to her. You can tell who Joan is even from the far side of the church. She's the one with the big smile. In the Peace you will get a hug and a kiss that will make you feel like a megastar. She sings with her hands raised in praise and adoration. Her evident devotion to Christ is the catalyst for others. Hymns of praise take off when Joan is around.

Joan has a pile of worship tapes and there's nearly always one playing in the car. She likes books with a devotional slant and last year read Henri Nouwen's *Return of the Prodigal* four times. The Bible is precious to her. She reads it most days, taking one or two verses at a time and chewing on them slowly. It's honey in her mouth. Joan smiles easily and is warm and approachable. She has a group of friends who meet to share and pray together. If anyone is a friend of Christ it's Joan.

One morning, in her prayer time, Joan read John 15. She was struck by a theme that came out of the page as if she'd never seen it before. *You will remain in my love if you obey my commands. My command is this, that you love one another. Greater love has no one than this, that someone lay down their life for their friends.* Joan was not too happy about the word 'command'. She wanted love to be spontaneous and natural. 'Obey' and 'command' seemed to come from another direction – duty, law, formality – all the things that seemed cold about the church before she came to faith.

The nagging feeling wouldn't go away. Obey my command. Lay down your life. She thought about Christ's love – it went to the cross. It washed the disciples' feet. Reluctantly at a quarter past seven Joan laid out before her several possibilities that she had pushed to the side. For weeks they'd been asking for people to help make coffee after the service and wash up but at that point Joan liked to talk with her friends and check up on all the things they'd been praying for. Then they wanted someone to commit themselves to talking to visitors and newcomers but that's when Joan had fellowship. It would be hard work talking to strangers even though she knew she'd do it well. The rota for visiting old folk was always short of people – so was the drop-in centre for overseas students – and doing door-to-door collection for Christian Aid.

It was an uncomfortable time that morning. Joan left her prayers disturbed. So being a friend of Christ meant love for the stranger and the visitor, giving time to do practical jobs, hiding away in the kitchen when all the fun was out there in church, listening to Mrs Chamberlain tell her for the nine-teenth time about the death of her cat. So that's what laying down your life might mean. 'Oh all right, Lord,' said Joan, writing herself a reminder note and sticking it on the cupboard by the phone.

THE IMAGINARY FRIEND: IS IT ALL WISHFUL THINKING?

The image of Jesus as the friend who never leaves you in the lurch is an enormously attractive one. But it does raise some awkward questions. Put brutally, how do I know I'm not deceiving myself? How do I know friendship with Christ isn't just a convenient and reassuring fiction? There is a stage in many children's development when they go around talking to imaginary companions. A friend of mine told me of his daughter's active social life spent in the company, apparently, of two invisible friends called Aggers and Efferwus. Another friend recalls his rich association with two characters called Eggshell and Treetrunk. Most parents are indulgent, knowing that the phase will pass. What if friendship with Jesus is just a rather sophisticated example of the same tendency? Is Christ a kind of celestial Tinkerbell, doomed to vanish if I don't keep saying I believe in him? Have I got to keep on imagining him or he'll go out of existence? Must I keep his life-support system going with religious talk? And if my mind wanders, will he disappear?

Obviously, friendship with Christ cannot be exactly the same as human friendship. I remember one young Christian saying plaintively, 'They tell us that Christ is a friend as real as your schoolfriends. But it isn't like that!' As important as the differences, however, are the occasions when it *does* resemble human friendship. Christians often speak of 'a sense of presence'. At such moments the presence of Christ is so real that it seems preposterous, if not blasphemous, to argue about his existence.

Perhaps this sense of presence is an irreducible experience. When we speak about it to our sceptical friends or family they may look quizzical. But there is more to be said about discerning his presence. The gospel, as so often, is dauntingly straight about this: 'If you have ears to hear, then use them.' Thus Jesus uncompromisingly insists on the hearer's responsibility. On one occasion he refers to the crowds as having ears but not listening, having eyes which they don't open. Their ears are heavy, their eyes closed, their hearts grown dull and gross. All of which suggests that the sense of the presence of Christ may not come easily to those who are blasé or convinced it is an illusion. Jesus seems to be saying, 'Ponder, reflect, pray, think, seek, search with all your heart, wait on God. It is your responsibility to open yourself up to the possibilities.'

That is our side of the equation. Christ does his part as well. Cyril of Jerusalem put it memorably in a sermon: 'Let yourself be taken, for Jesus is angling for you.' In this way he joins both the language of demand (you have a responsibility to open yourself up to Christ if you want him to speak to you) and the language of grace (Jesus like the skilful fisherman, is angling for you). For when we wait on Christ, searching for him in an ambiguous world, in the labyrinth of ordinary experience, longing to meet him, listening for the whisper of his voice, then he responds to us in grace.

Jesus affirms those who want to know him as friend: 'To you it has been given to know the mysteries of the kingdom'; 'to you who have much will more be given and you will have abundance'; 'many prophets and righteous men longed to see what you see and did not see it'; 'blessed are your eyes for they see and your ears for they hear' (Matthew 13 *passim*). These are words of promise and hope that lead us to go on looking for Christ.

This may not satisfy those outside the charmed circle who want a knock-down argument to show that talking to Christ is more than talking to yourself. All friendships work on the same principle, however: intimacy is given in response to openness, friendliness and vulnerability. Few friendships thrive where one party is peremptory or demanding. Why should we expect friendship with Christ to work on a different model? He approaches us first but waits for our response. And those who work at the friendship find that they come to know him better and more deeply, until the thought that they might be manufacturing the whole thing seems less and less to fit their lived experience.

MAINTAINING THE FRIENDSHIP: PRACTISING HIS PRESENCE

We can accept the reality of friendship with Christ and yet still be grateful for help in what is traditionally known as 'practising his presence'. A teenager speaking of prayer said, 'I'm sitting there talking and he's not saying much.' Some years ago, John Benington wrote an account of the conversion of a number of working-class young men, telling their stories in *Culture, Class and Christian Beliefs.*[1] After a period within the Christian community most of the men dropped out. When they were followed up, Benington remarked on the frequency with which they mentioned the demands of abstract thought as a major cause for giving up. One concluded that he was not 'built to cope with all this brain' (p. 30). The problem for many

---

1 John Benington, *Culture, Class and Christian Beliefs*, London, Scripture Union, 1973.

was how to 'make Christ real'. The struggle was often defined in terms of mental conflicts: 'terrific struggle in my mind'; 'my mind was in a turmoil all the time' (p. 62). Even though I have argued that friendship with Christ touches reality and not *virtual* reality, we still need to work at it.

I have found that, like any other friendship, the relationship with Christ needs to be maintained. Friends talk to one another; that points us towards the importance of prayer. Talking, confiding, listening, being silent in the presence of the other are all part of what is entailed in being a friend. Prayer is the lifeblood of the friendship. Praise is a way of showing appreciation for who the friend is and what he does. Confession of sin ensures that the lines of friendship are kept open and not marred by acts of betrayal and disloyalty. Even though your mind may behave like a kangaroo on speed, keep praying. As with any other friendship, say sorry for drifting away, put the unruly thought down and return to the conversation. If you continue to wander, it's probably worth talking to Christ about the topic that's so intrusive. If all else fails, try praying with your eyes open. And don't worry about it. Jesus is not easily miffed.

There are a variety of imaginative methods to help us realize the presence of Christ. It is a common sight in Spain to see life-sized figures of Christ in churches. Crucifixes, life-sized or not, are another way of focusing. It was in front of a crucifix in San Damiano that St Francis received the command to rebuild the church. Icons, paintings, posters, pictures may help. A special chair in a quiet place will aid meditation, as will a lighted candle or a glass of wine and a loaf of bread. Many people pray next to an empty chair, since this makes it easier to imagine Christ at one's side.

Many actions are evocative. Kneeling is the obvious one, of course, but the gesture of opening a Bible or a prayer book is not unlike that of breaking bread. Going on 'an Emmaus walk' with or without another Christian will evoke a sense of the Christ who walks with you. The Eucharist invites you to kneel and hold out empty hands; the body's movement itself confirms the relationship. Celtic spirituality made use of 'breastplate prayers' – while putting on one's clothes, one put on Christ. The Celts also developed the habit of bringing Christ into the most mundane tasks, lighting the fire, milking the cow – or we might say, doing the washing up, putting out the rubbish bin.

In all these practices the imagination is engaged without a flight into the non-rational. In his commentary on John's gospel, Barrett observes that there is an intellectual content to the faith that implies that Christians will use their minds and will resist being overwhelmed by emotionalism or swallowed up by mysticism. 'The way to God, the truth and the life are nowhere to be found if not in the historic, carnal reality of Jesus.'[2] This means that reflection on the portrait of Jesus as we have it in the gospels is an important part of maintaining the friendship with the living Christ. I shall say more about the practice of *lectio divina* in a later chapter.

I want to suggest one other method. Jesus is encountered in the faces of those we meet. In the story of the road to Emmaus (Luke 24:13–33) a meal is given new depth through the way Luke shapes the narrative: Jesus joins two disconsolate disciples on the road away from Jerusalem. He explains how all that has happened has been foreshadowed in the scriptures. Their hearts 'burn within them' but they fail to recognize Jesus, even in his words. It is not until the *meal* begins that their eyes are opened. In other words, there was no encounter in depth with the risen Lord until he sat down with them at table and broke the bread. The literal meaning of the word 'companion' is one who eats with you; this points us towards a Christ who is real, who is alive and well, and sitting in our living room.

This insight could transform our meals with friends. Grace at the start of meals can often be a perfunctory affair. What might it mean to our experience of the meal if we paused at the

2 C. K. Barrett, *The Gospel according to St John*, London, SPCK, 2nd edn, 1978, p. 85.

beginning to recollect the presence of Christ at the table? Then all meals, not just the five-course feast prepared at length with the aid of the Blessed Delia but also the takeaways, the curries and the deep-pan pizzas, all can be occasions when Christ eats with us. We meet him in the words and faces of friends; once again he makes himself known in the breaking of the bread.

THE SOCIETY OF FRIENDS: THE CHURCH'S EARLY WARMING SYSTEM

The friendliness of Jesus has the power to draw us and others to him. Among his opponents he acquired the reputation of being 'a gluttonous man and a winebibber', the friend of tax collectors and sinners, a man who enjoyed a party. This aspect of his character was demonstrated dramatically (and offensively) by his willingness to go as a guest to the house of anyone who invited him. In the Middle East eating with someone carried enormous symbolic significance. Jesus was open about his offer of friendship – he'd go anywhere.

Can the church let some of this friendliness escape? We often seem to want to keep 'our special friend' locked away. I'm interested in seeing how the friendly style of living showed itself in the life of the early church: in eating meals in one another's homes; in sharing news about one another (observe Paul's desire to know what has been going on in a congregation and his habit of passing on news about himself and his assistants); in bearing one another's burdens; in showing mutual respect and at times in voluntarily being subordinate to another; in not insisting on one's rights; in keeping no score of wrongs; in forbearance and putting up with one another's foibles and irritating quirks.

Can we reproduce any of this? There is something instantly warming about the Quakers' self-description as 'The society of friends'. The church should operate on the principle that 'any friend of Jesus is a friend of mine'. '[God's] love is made complete in us' (1 John 4:12) is a bold statement but one that is to be taken seriously.

For example, every congregation contains those who have been damaged by abusive family relationships. Often they behave in a socially dysfunctional way, bruising themselves and alienating others in the process. Sometimes they can be helped by professional counselling. But many only really learn what family life might be like, what relationships entail, how to behave maturely and non-manipulatively towards others when they encounter the robust, accepting friendship of adults who will play the part of loyal and supportive friends. Such a network of care can support others whom life has damaged – the bereaved, the lonely and the isolated. The society of Christ's friends completes the friendship of Christ.

What about those outside the church community? Ideally, the friends of Jesus should communicate his attractiveness to a society that is desperate for the friend who will never let them down. Unfortunately, the church sometimes fails to manage even the most superficial signs of friendliness and what might, in other contexts, be called 'customer care'. How many have rejected the church because a wedding was conducted in a perfunctory way, or a funeral service gabbled through at top speed? If someone tries out a church for the first time and no one speaks to them, why ever would they wish to return? A work colleague told me of a visit his mother made to church, while her husband was ill. To her horror she heard his name mentioned in the prayers as one who had died that week. At the end of the prayers the minister picked up his list, squinted at it and said, 'Ah, sorry. All the dead are sick and all the sick are dead.' So that's all right then.

One pastor of a large Californian church says that newcomers will give a congregation ten minutes. He argues that at the end of that brief time they have made up their minds whether they belong and whether they will come again. Christian congregations should be no less friendly than the instructors at the local health club or the assistants at the supermarket checkout. If they can greet you with a cheery smile and a word of welcome ('but of course, they've been on a customer care course and they don't really mean it') then the congregation on a Sunday morning should be able to manage something similar. Or is it a case of, 'Ah, we are not hypocrites; we show our genuine feelings by looking hostile'?

To be more positive, we ought not to underestimate the power of 'little Christs' to mediate Christ to others. I think of a couple who came to church on the off chance and were bowled over by the kindness they received. Genuine friendliness leading to genuine friendship is still probably the most effective evidence of the reality of Christ's love. It communicates directly with the other person in a way that disarms suspicion. When Billy Graham first visited Britain, the columnist Cassandra (journalist William Connor) set up an interview with him, probably with the intention of exposing the evangelist's hypocrisy. The article ended memorably: 'Who would have thought that ordinary, honest friendliness would cudgel us sinners so damned hard.'

REFLECTION

'If I am to complain, let me complain to Christ on the cross.' How helpful is this comment of St Francis? How easy is it to be honest in our prayers?

How can we keep the balance between friendship with Christ and a cosy chattiness? Between praying with freedom and assuming he is at our beck and call?

The master shares his plans, intentions and outlook. If this is so, why do we find it so difficult to see what's really going on in the details of our lives?' How, in practice, do you go about discerning the mind of Christ?

What methods have you tried in order to 'realize the presence of Christ'?

DISCUSSION

Draw up a five-point 'Friendliness Charter' for your church. After six months, how will you find out if it is working?

MEDITATION

This method of meditation may be unfamiliar to you but it is one way of bringing Christ into the world of the imagination.

Imagine that Christ is standing at the door of your home. Invite him in. You start to take him through the house showing him where you live.

Suddenly you realize that this house is your life. You walk through long corridors and up grand staircases to upper floors. It seems to have many more rooms than you had thought.

Some of the rooms are locked. And here in this one room there is something you would rather Christ did not see. You stand there unsure of what to do. To open the door is to invite embarrassment or shame.

Look at the face of Christ – patient, serious, searching, generous and kind.

You take the key, unlock the door and open it wide. He looks in and sees everything. But he knew it all before. It doesn't matter. It's all right.

PRAYER

O Christ, you know all things.
You know the secrets of the heart, and the strain of a
    divided life.
Give us such a vision of yourself that our hearts may be
    set on you alone;
such security in your love that our lives may show forth
    the beauty of your peace. Amen.

CHAPTER 3

THE GENEROUS GIVER

The story found in John 6:1–15 is often called *The feeding of the five thousand* but in many ways its older title – *the multiplication of the loaves* – is more appropriate, because the narrative is at least partly about vast numbers. At the start, five thousand men, plus women and children, two hundred denarii of bread (mentioned and immediately dismissed), a boy with five barley loaves and two fish. At the other end all are satisfied and twelve baskets of scraps are collected. The figures are stated clearly enough.

Between these numbers, holding them together, is a mystery. 'He took the loaves, gave thanks, and gave the loaves to those lying down.' Then later, 'And likewise from the fish. As much as they wanted.' The middle of the story is like a video moment that goes through too quickly. We say, 'Did I miss something? Can we run that bit back again?' We would like the action replay, to have it in slow motion. Unfortunately for the curious, the action refuses to be freeze-framed; it remains a mystery that will not be penetrated. So the gospel writers present us with an elusive Christ, not to be caught on *Candid Camera*.

A GOD WHO DOESN'T KNOW WHEN TO STOP

The mystery doesn't hide the abundance of the gift, however. A previous generation loved to rationalize such miracle stories. One theory speculated that the crowds brought their sandwiches but concealed them until shamed by the boy's unselfishness. Another, that the meal was in the nature of a sacrament so that no one received more than a crumb, a mere taste upon the tongue.

If we live in the story we soon see that such explanations run counter to the evangelist's intention. 'Jesus then took the loaves, gave thanks, and distributed to those who were seated *as much as they wanted.*' John does not intend us to imagine 'a little something'. Jesus gave and gave and gave and gave and gave. On and on and on and on and on. Bread came streaming from him. *As much as they wanted*. Use your imagination, says John. Four rows back a man was heard to complain, 'All I said was, *I feel a bit peckish*, and all this bread came at me. I can't handle it.' They were filled. Bread came in abundance, overflowing, a divine excess, a cornucopia of bread. In this extraordinary story of the inexhaustible supply of bread, pressed down, good measure and running over, John intends that we shall catch a glimpse of the sheer prodigality of Jesus. This is the Christ who gives life as God gives life.

Suddenly we are projected into the presence of a divine Mozart spinning symphonies of bread from his finger tips. Here is a God of soft-centred chocolates by the crate full, a God who fills the Sinai desert with quails to a depth of two and half feet and covers the face of the earth with manna. We stand in the presence of the Creator, who says, 'Let there be bread,' and there is bread. The same power that made the teeming earth with all its multimillion varieties of living things is here on a Galilean hillside! As if that were not enough, John continues in dead-pan tones, *He did the same with the fish*. As much as they wanted! The line from the hymn 'Cwm Rhondda' catches the mood – 'Bread of heaven, feed me till I want no more!' – the lavish, superabundant, limitless, extravagant generosity of Christ.

INTOXICATING EXTRAVAGANCE

There is something wildly exhilarating about a God who doesn't know when to stop. The Bible consistently offers us this picture. From the hand of God pour flowers and fruit, all living things, those that swarm in the depths of the sea, walk upon the land or fly in the air. The psalmist goes into overdrive:

You care for the land and water it;
you enrich it abundantly ...

You drench its furrows and level its ridges;
you soften it with showers and bless its crops.
You crown the year with your bounty,
and your carts overflow with abundance.
The grasslands of the desert overflow;
the hills are clothed with gladness.
The meadows are covered with flocks
and the valleys are mantled with corn;
they shout for joy and sing. (Psalm 65:9a,10–13)

God's basic nature is to be extravagant, bountiful, the giver of all good things.

In the gospels this God is embodied in Jesus. His actions are paradigms or models of what God is like. That is why he demonstrates the same extravagance as the God of the Old Testament. All four gospels contain accounts of miraculous feedings, with overtones of the manna that fed the Israelites in the desert. In his conversation with the woman of Samaria (John 4:10–14) Jesus promises living water that will ensure that she never thirsts again. Three chapters later he visits Jerusalem at the feast of Tabernacles and cries out, 'Whoever believes in me ... streams of living water will flow from within him' (John 7:37–9). Luke and John both record extraordinary catches of fish, so vast that the nets begin to break (Luke 5:1–11; John 21:1–14). The first of the signs by which Jesus 'manifested his glory' takes place at a wedding where, as supplies run out, the water in six stone jars is turned into the best wine of the feast (John 2:1–13).

This last story is preachers' delight. They love to calculate the volume of wine involved. Thomas Troeger[1] goes for 150

---

1 Thomas Troeger, *Ten Strategies for Preaching in a Multi-Media Culture*, Nashville, Abingdon Press, 1996, p. 24.

gallons and Fleming Rutledge[2] translates the figure into 2,160 glasses. What is it that tweaks the imagination? As Rutledge says, 'Twenty-one hundred glasses of the finest vintage for one little wedding party in a backwater village! What does this mean?' We are overwhelmed by the extravagance of the response to a minor problem. Jesus seems to have no idea of what would be sensible, within reasonable limits, sufficient without excess. Whatever would you do with all that wine? There's something irresponsible about such prodigality. The potential for drunkenness, horse-play and goodness knows what hanky-panky is enormous. It's all very well helping out in a domestic crisis, but God, of all people, ought to stop before everyone ends up under the table.

THE ECONOMICS OF HEAVEN

The three model miracles – of water into wine, feeding the multitudes and the catches of fish – point towards a Christ who embodies divine generosity, even excess: there is too much wine; the nets break; there are twelve baskets of scraps. If Jesus is, in David Jenkins's phrase, 'the man God chose to be', then his words and deeds imply a surprisingly, exhilaratingly and intoxicatingly extravagant God. This really is amazing grace.

We are too familiar with the theme to notice. Key passages have become dulled by constant repetition so that we find it difficult to feel their shocking nature. But look again at the parables. God is a shepherd who leaves the ninety-nine sheep 'on the hills' and goes in search of the one that has wandered off (Matthew 18:12–14). Jesus' innocent question 'Will he not leave the ninety nine?' invites the prudent answer 'No, he will not! Only a fool would do such a thing.'

---

2 Fleming Rutledge, *The Bible and the New York Times*, Grand Rapids, MI, William B. Eerdmans Publishing Company, 1998, pp. 71–2.

The parable of the unforgiving debtor begins with the breathtaking picture of a king who sets aside a debt of 10,000 talents (Matthew 18:21–35). The exaggeration is deliberate, like a cartoon. A talent was worth 6,000 denarii and a denarius was a day's wages for a labourer. So the debt comes to 60 million denarii – a sum beyond imagination. It's worth noting that in one year the total tax income from the regions of Judaea, Samaria and Idumaea only came to 600 talents. No doubt 10,000 talents made the listeners' heads ache in the same way that billions of dollars do ours. And yet, this debt is cancelled at a stroke by a king who clearly doesn't understand economics.

With this in mind we are not surprised to find a householder who does everything in his power to ensure that his house is full of guests when he holds a feast (Luke 14:15–24); or a father who, despite having been grossly insulted by his son, still insists on throwing a lavish party for his son when he decides to return home (Luke 15:11–32).

The parable of the talents begins with a wealthy landowner turning over the management of all his property to his servants (Matthew 25:14). What a risky move – trusting his servants enough to trust them with his future. But here is a master who trades riskily and lives dangerously. He is prepared to be vulnerable, to set aside the possibility of financial disaster in the interests of partnership. Foolhardy, ill advised, improvident, extravagant? Whatever did we expect?

However, the story of the labourers in the vineyard (Matthew 20:1–15) is the touchstone of our understanding of a God who is all grace. Those who have worked all day are paid the exact amount for which they were contracted. There is no injustice on the part of the vineyard owner. But, scandalizing those who worked the longest (and incidentally scandalizing generations of good church people), the owner pays the same wages to those who began only at the very close of the working day. It's not fair. No it's not, but it's marvellous!

It is, of course, natural for us to line up with those who assume that the show runs on the lines of tit for tat and are cross when others profit from a breach in the standard arrangements. However, when we stand in the place of those who have hung around the market place all day, we feel differently. Constantly passed over, having nothing that will make us employable, we are suddenly overwhelmed by a generosity we have done nothing to deserve. We are touched by the divine fire. The author of the fourth gospel exclaims, 'From the fulness of his grace we have all received one blessing after another' (John 1:16). Even so.

Do we Believe it? No Such Thing as a Free Lunch

Do we believe it? This may seem a very strange question indeed, but experience inclines me to ask it just the same. Grace is not always easy to accept. The gospel always contains an element of 'it is just too good to be true'. But that's God for you. In Anne Holm's novel, *I Am David*, the boy David escapes from a prison camp, presumably in an iron curtain country. He starts to make his way across Europe hoping to get back to Denmark where he believes he will find his mother. En route he is 'befriended' by a dog, which David insists is a free dog, since he has seen enough of coercion and compulsion in the camp. David insists that King, the dog, has chosen to go with him.

Towards the end of the book David hides from a party of men with guns – we are told very little about them but are led to believe that they constitute a threat to the boy's safety. Just before David's hiding place is discovered, the dog breaks cover and seems to run at the men quite deliberately. We hear a cry of pain and then a shot. In that moment David realizes that the dog is distracting their attention from him and succeeds in making his escape.

This scene takes on added significance when it is set against David's view of God. At the beginning of his journey David chooses the 'God of the still waters and green pastures' to be his God, knowing nothing about him except that he was once associated with someone called David. The relationship is a fragile one, however, since David admits that he can do nothing for God and everyone knows that you cannot get something for nothing. The incident with the dog changes David's perception.

> Its very bark as it sprang forward had seemed to say, 'Run, run!' And all the while David was running, he had known he must not turn back and try to save it. He must not let the dog's action be in vain: he had to accept it. So one could get something for nothing after all?[3]

The lesson that you can get something for nothing when you deal with God is not an easy one to learn. Many church members will believe in their heads that God is gracious but fail to feel it in their hearts. Unfortunately, it is possible to live one's Christian life entirely at the level of the head, 'knowing' that he is loving and generous yet vaguely uneasy with the idea.

A dramatic example of this appears in Gerard Hughes's *God of Surprises*. Hughes was running a retreat for a group that included 'Fred', considered to be 'a model Christian'. He encouraged him to meditate on scenes from the gospels, suggesting on one occasion that he picture Jesus at the marriage at Cana of Galilee. At the end of the day in question, Fred reported, describing in vivid terms the tables heaped with food, the dancing and general merriment. 'Did you see Christ?' asked Hughes. 'Yes,' he said. 'Christ was sitting upright on a straight-backed chair, clothed in a white robe, a staff in his hand, a crown of thorns on his head, looking disapproving.'[4] It is possible to talk convincingly about a God of mercy but live a life dominated by guilt and driven by a Deity who never lets up.

---

3 Anne Holm, *I Am David*, (trans. L. W. Kingsland), Harmondsworth, Puffin Books, 1969, p. 149.
4 Gerard Hughes, *God of Surprises*, London, Darton, Longman and Todd, 1985, p. 36.

A less dramatic but equally revealing example was told to me by a young woman. She had a vivid dream in which she found herself walking the Via Dolorosa watching Christ as he carried his cross to Calvary. As she told the story, she 'felt fed up and depressed and burdened down with all my problems'. She said, 'It was as if I was carrying shopping bags full of them. Suddenly I was aware of Jesus turning towards me and saying, "Let me have those". "Oh no," I said. "You've got more than enough to carry already."' Most of us can understand the impulse to give Jesus a helping hand. We can sing about casting our cares on the Lord but still find it extremely difficult to accept deep down that he cares for us in the unreserved, no-small-print way the hymns go on about. But grace is God's very essence. It's what he's made of; it's what he's good at.

Does the World Believe it?
Quid pro Quo and Tit for Tat

We might suppose that extravagance on this scale would be instantly attractive to those outside the church. Oddly enough, however, our society is suspicious about generosity. For a start, people do not trust it. They are jumpy when they encounter free offers. It is axiomatic that there is no such thing as a free lunch. 'What's she after?' 'It must be a publicity stunt.' 'Is he trying to buy my vote, sell me insurance, or trap me into a timeshare I don't want?' We've all been selected dozens of times by the Reader's Digest computer to go into the Final Draw for this month's star prize, the Porsche, the holiday in Bali or the new kitchen. It's just that Mrs Snodgrass of Bridlington always wins. The only sensible, hard-headed question to ask is, 'What's the catch?' To the cry 'O ye of little faith' the proper response is 'O me of much experience.'

People not only mistrust generosity; they also feel that there is something destabilizing about it. We have all met people who won't let us do anything for them – they can cope; they don't like being done good to; they like to stay in charge.

It is interesting to observe how often talking of free forgiveness and grace will produce a similarly vigorous protest. Sometimes the objection is that this is not authentic Christianity. Simply, it cannot be true. Then, when you insist that it is, they reply that, in that case, there is something deeply flawed about it. If forgiveness is free and does not need to be earned, then what is to stop people taking God for a ride and milking the system? A friend said to me years ago, 'It can't be right to live how you want for eighty years and file a quick repentance in the last few minutes before death.' Getting the star prize, without having worked for it, may be fine for the National Lottery but it is not, and ought not to be, the way the world is made.

Put this way, grace is not just amazing, it is also scandalous. We won't be surprised, however, if we remember the gospels. In Palestinian society, Jesus' habit of eating with anyone who would have him was a stumbling block to many. If the world does not belong to the respectable, the upright, the moral and the good living, if all those years of doing your best, paying your dues, and keeping your nose clean count for nothing, if tax collectors and prostitutes enter the kingdom before the righteous, then people will take gross advantage (as they always do) and the fabric of society will be undermined. The whining and bleating elder brother in the parable of the prodigal son usually carries the sympathy vote.

This attitude underpins the conventional view of Christianity. Even though God is the God in whom people do not believe, everyone knows that he runs the universe like a bank. Over the years you make deposits, a donation to Oxfam here, a kind word to an unattractive relation there. Every little helps. Withdrawals come in the form of the odd swear word, getting drunk, road rage and meddling with your neighbour's wife. When time is called God checks the status of the current account and if you are in the black you appear at the Pearly Gates before St Peter who checks immigration details and allows access. Those whose account is in the red go down to 'the other place', to be tormented by demons in red tights with toasting forks. No one seriously believes the details of this picture – it is after all, the subject of innumerable jokes and cartoons – but many believe the assumptions that lie beneath this picture. That's the way, more or less, how God manages human destiny. God runs the universe on a profit and loss basis. He can't be that generous.

We can see this underlying assumption coming to the surface in what people say when they're taken unawares. Two largely implicit beliefs jostle one another. We might call the first 'You gotta pay your dues', and it goes like this: Into every life a certain amount of rain must fall. You can take avoiding action and perform various rituals to ward off the showers, but the universe is geared to exacting some payment for allowing you the privilege of living on the planet and getting by with a relatively happy life.

The second comes into play when things go wrong. Then it is common to ask, 'What have I done to deserve this?', as if bad behaviour carried a tariff – much like a motoring offence – and the moral equivalent of minor infringements of the speeding laws had suddenly been met with a lifetime ban. I remember reading the transcript of an interview with a man whose subterranean creed consisted of 'If I do my duty and play fair by everyone, then I shall be all right.' Sadly, the interview was part of a study of redundancy. It was painful to read his bewilderment and sense of betrayal. He had done his duty and played fair, and suddenly towards the end of his working life he found himself without a job. Why wasn't the universe paying out? It was as if he had faithfully paid his pension contributions only to discover that some unnoticed clause in the small print had made him ineligible to draw on the fund.

The code of social interaction that follows from this standpoint assumes that it is prudent to live by looking out for family and friends – an ethic of sensible, limited reciprocity. Friends and family will then look out for us when the rainy day arrives. It is an ethic of 'You scratch my back and I'll scratch yours.' Jesus described it as the common-sense way of living: loving those who love you; greeting those who are your brothers (Matthew 5:46,47). In other words, that's normal; you know it makes sense: 'Even the tax collectors and the pagans do that.'

What is not normal and what may seem, depending on your point of view, radical, attractive, scandalous, wonderfully idealistic or plain stupid is to follow the example of God, the heavenly Father, who indiscriminately causes his sun to rise on the evil and the good and sends rain on the righteous and the unrighteous.

CAN WE LIVE IT? TRYING TO START AN EPIDEMIC

What would happen if the church consisted of men and women who had been infected by the divine generosity and couldn't help spreading it around? Once past the initial check-point of suspicion, it is a quality that carries its own authority. It doesn't need the support of argument; it has its own magnetic power and is enormously attractive.

Generosity works miracles. Last year I saw the film *Babette's Feast* for the first time. I found it profoundly moving. It is set in a narrow, pietistic rural community in nineteenth-century Denmark. Babette, a refugee from Paris, has been taken in by two sisters and has become the family cook. Both sisters have in their different ways stifled and denied their gifts and talents and now live lives of rectitude, commendable but restricting.

Unbeknown to the sisters Babette wins 10,000 francs in the lottery and decides to use the whole amount to cook a meal such as no one in the community could ever have experienced. The meal is indeed beyond all imagining and we watch in fascination as the group of twelve sitting round the table are transformed. At first they are stiff and correct, determined not to enjoy what they are eating. Then they begin to relax; conversation eases; there is laughter and appreciative words, confession of long-held grudges, apologies and a rediscovery of community and friendship. It is no exaggeration to say that the group rediscovers life through the meal. Towards the end of the film we discover that Babette was once the head chef at the famous Café Anglais in Paris.

The parallels with the grace of God are easy to draw. Babette gave a lifetime of skill at enormous cost to the one project of cooking a meal that would transform the lives of those who ate it. The guests at her table were overwhelmed and transformed by her abundant generosity.

Jesus' all-inclusive meals are a good example of the drawing power of hospitality. As far as we can tell, no one was turned away. Barriers came down, tongues were loosened and in the process lives were changed. We can see this clearly in Matthew's account of a meal at Bethany (Matthew 26:6–12). While Jesus is at table a woman comes in with an alabaster jar of very expensive perfume. She pours it over his head in an extravagant gesture. The disciples, as we have come to expect, hold to the common-sense view. They are indignant at the waste involved. They propose alternative uses for the perfume (apparently forgetting that it was not theirs). It could have been sold for a good price and the money devoted to charitable purposes. All very sensible – and worthy and dull and so PC you could scream. But the heart that has been touched by the grace of Christ cannot be prudent and careful.

Nor can you *prescribe* for the heart that has been touched by the grace of Christ. The woman decides that Jesus shall have it all, and hang the expense. I remember a churchwarden saying to me about her church's appeal, 'We personally can't afford our donation but it's only money.' I was recently enormously encouraged by a Christian professor of economics, who whispered to me conspiratorially during a discussion on finance, 'Sometimes I think the church should waste money.' These are some of the signs of hearts warmed by grace, breaking out of the straitjackets of what is normal and expected, marked by the freakiness and playfulness of the gospel.

How else can you explain American minister Tony Campolo's habit of paying for the car behind him at toll gates? As far as I can tell the motorists who benefit from these acts of generosity will never meet Campolo and will probably not know why they have been chosen. Similarly, how do you account for the members of one Canadian congregation who go around feeding parking meters which are about to expire! You might think that there are more useful things to do with the money. These random acts of kindness are not performed for utilitarian reasons – to impress people or improve the image of the church – but, exuberantly, for the sheer pleasure of knowing that this is God's style. He gets equally carried away with the joy of giving.

Perhaps we need to look again at the extravagance of Christ. The Nazareth sermon (Luke 4:24–9) invited the hearers to see his ministry through the framework of the Year of Jubilee. But if you look up the regulations for the Year of Jubilee in Leviticus 25 you will find that it was an economically preposterous arrangement when debts were cancelled and those whose labour (and bodies) were mortgaged to their owners were permitted to go home.

God's generosity calls sound economics into question. In Luke 10:35 the good Samaritan writes a blank cheque for the innkeeper: 'I will reimburse you for any extra expense you may have.' 'Never sign blank cheques,' says the voice of the realist.

According to the teaching of Jesus, disciples are to forgive the enemy, turning the cheek when they are assaulted. When they are asked for their coat they are to give their cloak as well. If a Roman soldier commands them to carry his pack for one mile, they are to offer to carry it for a second. They must give to those who ask for a handout and lend to those who want to borrow from them (Matthew 5:38–45; Luke 6:27–37). This kind of thing is so manifestly a recipe for being ripped off and exploited that we are not surprised to find that the church, down the years, has shrewdly turned the commands into 'illuminating and challenging suggestions'. But the generous style of life is catching.

We may feel that there are many less dramatic ways in which we can express divine generosity. For example, to forgive someone who injures you seventy times seven (Matthew 18:21–2) may be beyond our powers, but churches, neighbourhoods and families are full of people who have not yet managed to forgive once. Christ says, 'Why not begin there and work up to the other 489?' To let a grudge go is an act of generosity. It's so much more comforting to hug it to you, polishing it from time to time in order to keep it bright and shiny.

No doubt there is a need for balance. Ministers who give freely to everyone who comes to the door are taken for a ride. There will be many occasions when a meal voucher is wiser than a sentimental financing of a drug habit or drink problem. Open churches lose all their silver and so on and so on. But does prudence have to be the last word? The church has the reputation of always asking for money. I happen to think that this is not true. Nevertheless I am impressed to hear of churches that decline to pass the plate round in case they should reinforce the folk myth. One church distributed the video of Jesus of Nazareth around their neighbourhood. They gave it away free. It was interesting to hear how many recipients were unable to believe that anything was being given away with no strings attached. So often discussions in the Anglican Church about the Parish Share turn into competitions about who can get away with giving least. One diocesan secretary said to me, 'I long for the day when somebody says, "Can we give more?" ' Is it so impossible for us to recapture the sheer hysteria of giving?

Generosity shows itself in dozens of other ways as well. We have all valued the generosity of someone's time, the gift that is involved when someone listens attentively and without judgement. Phone calls 'just to check how things are', the wonderfully flexible e-mail, cards and notelets, notes of encouragement and support, the loan of books, newspaper cuttings – the television advert gives us the nudge: 'I saw this and thought of you.' Hospitality in one's home, whether it's a four-course meal or a takeaway and a video, is in the style of Christ. Generosity does not have to cost 10,000 francs.

In an unpublished study of 'Generation X' (those born between 1964 and 1984), Ted Schroder says that that generation is looking for a community to belong to and to call home, even though at the same time they can be deeply cynical about community. He comments, 'Exercising hospitality means creating time and space in your life. It means sharing meals and letting people into our comfort zones.' It is fascinating to speculate on the success of the Alpha enterprise, one of the most productive evangelism initiatives of the last decade. Surely at least part of its attractiveness to the person who would not dream of coming into a church is the fact that the organizers allowed themselves to be taught by Christ: at the heart of the Alpha philosophy is a common meal.

These are just a few of the directions in which we may be led by the grace of God. When I asked at random in my church how generosity might show itself in ordinary life, one woman answered immediately, 'When cars are waiting at side roads trying to get out into the queue of traffic, let them get out in front of you.' There is no end to the possibilities.

I went recently to give an address at a conference centre in Yorkshire. The organizer showed me to my room. I was surprised to see a chocolate bar on the pillow. 'What's this?' I said. 'It's for you,' came the reply. 'Does everyone get one?' 'Oh, yes.' Further inquiry uncovered the fact that he had phoned the wives, husbands and friends of the conference participants to find out their favourite brand of chocolate bar. As he left the room he said, 'And they'll all get another one tomorrow. Oh, by the way, there's an iced gateau for you in the fridge.'

THE GENEROUS CHRIST

In a world like ours grace and generosity can have an amazing impact. Through us the generous extravagance of Christ can be made real. 'Everyone shafts you in business,' said Nasty Nick Bateman, the unfortunate villain of the television show *Big Brother*. Against that background people can encounter a Christ who offers to eat with them (an act of friendship) and have them home to his place (an act of generosity). In a litigious society, where, if there's blame there's a claim, it is refreshing just to meet people who will not insist on their rights or take you to the small claims court. It's even better if they will do something for nothing. Such grace is both attractive and powerful and is referred to in the New Testament as, loosely translated, 'super-mega-hyper-abundant' (Ephesians 3:20). Can even a bit of it be embodied in us?

REFLECTION

To what aspects of your life, both present and past, do you point when you want to name the grace and generosity of God?

In what ways have you, over the past few weeks, been the recipient of the generosity and grace of other people? How do you feel about this? How do you feel towards them? How easy is it to receive grace from others? Do you feel a need to pay it back?

Spend some time thinking of those who have expressed the generosity of God towards you since you were a child to the present day. Try to recall specific incidents. Thank God for their kindness.

Letting go of a grudge is an act of generosity. Is there someone you know you ought to forgive?

Look at one of the parables listed in the section above 'The Economics of Heaven' (pages 40–42). Where do you see yourself in the story? Run through the story again, imagining yourself as one of the characters.

DISCUSSION

In what specific ways does your church model the generosity of God – both towards its members and those outside in the community? Can you think of other ways in which it could embody God's generosity?

Plan an act of generosity for the coming week. When you meet next week, share what happened.

Prayer

Lord of generosity and grace,
I offer you my pain and confusion,
My pettiness and unwillingness to forgive,
My hesitant and faithless prayers,
My stammering and faltering speech,
My plans and projects,
My abilities – such as they are.

I can do nothing but pray for my friend,
I can do nothing but bring this situation to you,
I can do nothing but ask that you will touch me with
    your Spirit,
I can do nothing but come to your table with empty
    hands ...

And you multiply the loaves and give me grace upon
    grace,
Filling me with the Bread of Life.

CHAPTER 4

THE BOUNDARY VIOLATOR

If you want to live in an orderly world, you need to put things in boxes. From time to time my wife and I engage in an activity known as 'sorting the kitchen out'. The contents of the drawers and cupboards are rationalized according to an elegant blueprint that goes something like this: 'Knives, forks, spoons go just here, larger ones on the left down to teaspoons on the right. In this drawer, cling film and smaller bin liners. The cupboard below the sink will take washing-up liquid, tablets for the dishwasher, dusters and Domestos. Above the cupboard will be stored the cat food, along with cat biscuits. Tins for the humans, both savoury and sweet, will go here in this cupboard. On the wall a rack of herbs for cooking. Everything that's needed for breakfast over here.' This done, we look at one another with deep satisfaction and firm resolve: 'Now! Do you think we can keep to this system? It makes for happy cooks and a happy kitchen.' We really should get out more.

'Dirt is matter in the wrong place,' wrote the anthropologist Mary Douglas. There is no dirt in the garden. When dirt is in the garden we call it 'soil' or 'a fine tilth'. It becomes dirt when it gets on the new carpet. What turns it from 'soil' to 'dirt' is the fact that it has crossed a boundary. It's moved out of one box or category into another. The boundary is somewhere around the front door, although there is a no man's land of the porch where soil exists uneasily. In this limbo land between garden and house it suspects it might be in the process of becoming 'dirt', but has not yet experienced the undignified sweeping up into the dustpan and ignominious expulsion from the house that will signify that it's soil again.

Boxes, boundaries and categories have power to name, and thus create, a world.

Form-filling is an exercise in defining through boundaries. We are classified by name, address, postcode, gender, age, salary, and so on. What began as a whole person is divided up into categories. The individual is dissected and reappears in a different guise. Some characteristics are highlighted because they are relevant to the purposes of those who designed the form. Other characteristics that may be of intense importance to the individual are marginalized or even become invisible. For this particular form no one wants to know that you can sing all the words of 'American Pie' or that you have a tattoo of a dragon in an unusual place – or even that Lloyd George knew your father. Your beautiful, undivided self is reallocated into boxes and the self is not always in control of the process.

Most of the time this is a necessary way of dealing with the complicated bundles of attributes that make up individuals. Occasionally it is irritating. Market research is particularly provoking. My wife answered the phone to a cold-caller trying to sell double glazing. The opening remark was 'Can I speak to your husband?' She was clearly on the wrong side of someone else's boundary, in the category labelled 'Not male'. Sometimes the only category of interest to the assistant who sells you the camera, once the credit card details have been given, is your postcode. Decisions about design and distribution, about advertising and marketing will be made on the basis of where people like you live. I suppose that's all right, but when your car insurance goes up entirely because of your postcode, you might want to redraw the boundary or argue that your twenty years of accident-free motoring is much more relevant than where you happen to live.

A World of Lines Drawn in the Sand

The biblical world was very similar. People of Jesus' day lived in a world of boundaries. There were boundaries for food – kosher and non-kosher. So cows were in and pigs were out. Meat and milk were not to be mixed. Chicken was in; hoopoe, bat and osprey were out. Locust, cricket and grasshopper were on the acceptable side of the line, while gecko, skink and chameleon were beyond the pale. There were boundaries for places: the temple courts were a map of areas of different degrees of holiness – the court of the Gentiles, the court of women, the court of the Levites and so on until at the very centre, the cleanest space of all, the Holy of Holies. But even the land itself was marked off from all other lands. Israel lay on this side of the boundary; foreign lands were outside the circle. So pious Jews on re-entering Israel would brush the dust of alien territory off their sandals. The Jewish historian Josephus records that Herod had great difficulty in finding Jews who were prepared to live in Tiberias, because the soil was defiled. There were boundaries for people, so that some trades, like shepherds and tanners, were on the wrong side of the line. Some classes of people were similarly excluded. The gospels give many examples of social boundaries that shut out whole groups, like Gentiles, tax collectors, women and Samaritans. Even eating with such people was risky. And then there were those other dangerous elements – blood, bodily emissions, menstruation, childbirth, death, dirt and disease. All these came from the dark side; they polluted and contaminated the ordered world.

The gospels reflect a society criss-crossed with boundaries, a world of lines drawn to include and exclude, to classify and categorize. No doubt the grid was carried about in the brain so that every situation, whether it involved food, days of the week, people or places, was almost instantly configured according to the mental map. Proper insulation was required. It was well to keep a safe distance from anything contagious. We of the twenty-first century have no reason to feel superior. We also have our maps of what's in and what's out.

Easier to Raise the Dead

In the Palestine of Jesus' day, everyone was agreed: lepers were placed outside the circle of purity. The medical term for modern leprosy is Hansen's disease, a curable affliction. Biblical leprosy seems to have covered any skin complaint. It included such conditions as psoriasis, ringworm and lupus. It may even have been applied to mould on fabrics or mildew on walls. However, it is less important for us to identify the precise condition in each case of biblical leprosy as to understand the social consequences of being a leper.

Leprosy lay far beyond the boundary that divided cleanness and uncleanness. Those suffering from leprosy had to cover their mouths, wear their hair unkempt, and live away from towns and villages. At the approach of a healthy person, they had to shout 'Unclean! Unclean!' Lepers did not get cured. Perhaps a few recovered naturally and mysteriously and, in theory, spontaneous cures were possible; however, the focus of concern was not on curing but on protecting the rest of society. The priest was a kind of medical officer of health, responsible for diagnosis.

In the circumstances, to hear the dreaded words 'You have leprosy!' must have been like a death sentence. In cases of remission, after careful scrutiny, some might be given the formal certification that was their passport to re-enter society. Generally though, the proverb summed it up well enough: 'To heal a leper is more difficult than to raise the dead.' In fact, the rabbis said the cleansing of lepers would be a sign of the age of the Messiah. For the moment there was little to be done except make sure that lepers lived outside the village, giving healthy people plenty of warning, so that nobody ran the risk of catching anything nasty.

One day, so Luke records (Luke 5:12–16), a man full of leprosy comes along and accosts Jesus *while he is in one of the towns*. The story grips me immediately. I want to know what Jesus will do. Jesus is in the town and a man riddled with leprosy approaches him. Now here is a flagrant boundary violation. The man has already done the unforgivable. How dare he enter a town, putting every healthy person at risk! We gather from the story that he is desperate, since he falls with his face to the ground and begs Jesus for help; but even so ...

The leper's first words may seem odd to us. They suggest that the man is unsure of his reception. 'If you are willing,' he cries. Have you ever paused to ask why he should ask that question? Why ask Jesus about his willingness? What is there to doubt?

Presumably he asks because all his life he has been told that religious people are holy and clean. He knows that you 'look up to them' even though at this moment he has his face pressed to the ground. The holier they are the further they are removed, the better insulated, the more distant. And holiness, whether it's space or objects or people, seems so easily contaminated. This is an odd phenomenon, but he has been carefully taught that it is so – even a woman after childbirth can contaminate the temple courts and a dead body will pollute a rabbi. In fact, holy space, holy objects and holy people seem remarkably prone to catch whatever's going. The only safe course of action for a really holy person when encountering the unclean is to lift up his skirts and run like mad. As everyone knows, 'You cannot touch pitch without being defiled.' The unclean person will have to clean up first. Otherwise they will certainly pass their uncleanness on.

We assume without thinking that in the world of purity, the unclean will always pollute the clean. 'Put that down, Jimmy, you don't know where it's been' is sheer common sense. And yet there is something strange about the principle. Why does the traffic always have to be one way? Why does the clean never overwhelm the dirty? It was this principle that made lepers such a threat. Their diseased flesh came from the dark, seething, uncontrollable, chaotic world beyond, at the edges of the light. Lepers unsettled the established order of things.

So, 'If you are willing' – but there is every chance you might not be.

Beyond the Boundaries

More important than the medical use of the term is the way the word 'leper' is used to refer to anyone who is outside our boundary of safety and purity. The phrase 'I wouldn't touch him with a barge pole' is about keeping a safe distance. Our world has its own lepers and they have nothing to do with Hansen's bacillus.

We find the leper in those who are dirty, smelly or unkempt: the bag lady, the down and out, and the drunk. When information about AIDS first reached this country it was greeted with the sort of panic last seen at the time of the Black Death. The photograph of the Princess of Wales holding the hand of a dying man was a deliberate attempt to allay fear. Those who are socially inept become shunned at parties. Watch in a discussion group what happens to the person who rocks the boat with a remark that is too violent, too abrasive or too emotional. At coffee time they will drink alone. It is a common experience for bereaved people to say that they feel like lepers, especially when they see one-time friends cross the street so that they can avoid having to speak to them. The vigilante attacks on suspected paedophiles show how near the surface is the urge to purify the space where we live. We demonize groups that are different – those who look rough, or have very short haircuts, or accents that don't fit or body piercings. Or, to be fair, those who wear suits or speak in cut-glass tones, or ride to hounds or drink Pimms. The young insult and abuse the old – as they dodder along at 20 m.p.h. in the fast lane. The old fear and curse the young – randy as rabbits and idle as three-toed sloths. The list of lepers is a long one.

The Healing Touch

Against this background I watch with fascination to see what Jesus will do. I want to know how God incarnate treats those outside the pale.

He reached out his hand and touched the man.

He touched him. The man has violated a boundary. And Jesus responds by violating a boundary in his turn. His hand rests on the contaminated, contaminating flesh. The touch says everything that needs to be said, 'You are more important than any disease you've got.'

There is compassion here, certainly. But I don't feel that Jesus' action is patronizing or condescending. The touch is a statement of complete acceptance, straightforward, honest and real, without being theatrical about it. We see a hands-on God. The touch of Jesus becomes an icon of God and a sign for all those who are driven out into the wilderness by their own people. It also becomes an invitation to all who come after Jesus to do likewise. That invitation has been accepted by countless people, some famous – St Francis kissing the leper, the Duchess of Kent hugging sick children, Mother Teresa with her habit soiled with the marks of the dying – and others all unknown, who have touched, kissed, held, hugged, shared food with, sat with, listened to and cleaned up after, those who have been put on the wrong side of the boundary.

Jesus cleansed the man. He said, 'Be clean,' and he was. We would like it to be like that. And it often isn't. We know that this is a mystery we have to live with, though often it is hard to do so. Sometimes we discover that there is healing of damaged lives even when we cannot speak of a cure. And sometimes, gloriously, there is both healing and cure and then it is a sign of the age to come, when disease and distance will be no more. But common to all these experiences is the touch of God's hand – the hands-on God – who reaches across the gap we create.

Christ stretching out his hand is an image, a powerful metaphor worth praying deep into our consciousness. But I don't want to leave it as only a metaphor. Touch is always significant to us. In a world where we are crammed up against each other in the tube train, jostled in the rush hour and stamped on in the Sales, it is strange that we notice any physical contact. But intentional touch still communicates. Research has apparently demonstrated that even the touch of the assistant's fingers when giving the customer change at the checkout is noticed at a subliminal level.

How much more powerful is a reassuring hand on an arm, a cross traced in oil on the forehead, or holding the hand of someone in a coma. We know, of course, that touch can be a means of abuse and that indiscriminate hugs can turn the Peace into a nightmare for the sensitive soul. We know that, for some people, touch may evoke memories of past hurt. But, with all the qualifications, it would be a tragedy if Christians, through fear, left touching, with all its possibilities for healing, to the abuser, the groper or office lecher. Touch is a sign of Christ's grace, the symbol of his lovingkindness and the promise that one day all will be well. A song from the Iona community, 'The Touching Place', brings together the touch of Christ and the touch of his followers:

> To the lost Christ shows his face
> To the unloved he gives his embrace;
> To those who cry in pain or disgrace,
> Christ makes with his friends a touching place.[1]

TOUCHED WITH OUR INFIRMITIES

The emphasis up to this point has been on Jesus' action in touching the leper. He takes the initiative and remains in control. But we all know that there are situations where we are not in charge, where other people touch us and our response is a reaction to a move made by another.

I once took part in a Maundy Thursday foot washing. When the ceremony was over I reflected on what had taken place. My first thoughts were that something drastic happens to the symbolism of foot washing once it is transferred from the hot and dusty Middle East of the first century and transplanted to

---

1 John L. Bell and Graham Maule, 'The Touching Place', in *Love from Below*, Glasgow, Wild Goose Publications, 1989.

the chilly north of England in March. What was technically the same action changed meaning somewhere *en route*. Predictably, both I and the student who was my partner had washed our feet and changed our socks for the occasion. As I reflected on this it dawned on me that, in our society, having one's feet washed is considerably more threatening than washing someone's else's feet. Bare feet in a cold cathedral is a condition of vulnerability. We both felt better once we'd put our shoes and socks back on.

How Jesus reacts when he is touched is a powerful sign of how much he is able to make himself vulnerable and hand himself over to others. We see this at its most extreme in the Passion narrative when he is content to be handed over to sinful men, to be stripped, dressed in borrowed clothes and beaten. Hands that aim only to hurt and abuse are given free reign. One of the nastiest moments in the account of the mockery is when the soldiers blindfold him and pluck his beard. This is gratuitous spitefulness and we can only marvel that Jesus allowed it to be done to him. But in his willingness to be touched so brutally we see his strength and love.

Being touched is part of being vulnerable. It was a cause of scandal that a professed holy man should touch a leper. Just as significant is the reaction of Jesus when those considered to be unclean try to touch him.

Mark tells a story of a woman with a menstrual haemorrhage (Mark 5:25–34). She is permanently unclean and her touch will pass on impurity. But the power of the story is precisely that Jesus is passive: he is acted upon. She comes through the crowd, determined to touch him somehow or another, even if it is only the edge of his clothes. And having been touched without his permission, he does not react with anger or disgust. Even though a taboo has been broken by the woman, even though Jesus is ritually contaminated by her touch, the sheer glory and delight of this story is that he and the woman meet face to face, surrounded by men who haven't a clue what is really going on. The two meet; it is a real meeting and it ends in a joyful pronouncement, 'Go in peace'.

This episode has been sensitively retold from the woman's point of view by Jane Speck in an unpublished sermon:

The woman is ill. Her illness is personal, intimate, not the kind of thing one talks about. She has been ill for twelve years.

No one has touched her for twelve years.

Because of her illness, this woman must live apart from all others. If anyone should touch her, they are by law unclean. If anyone should sit on a stool or bed on which she has sat, they are then by law unclean.

This woman, sitting in her doorway and squinting down the road in front of her, used to have great wealth. Jewels and perfumes adorned her body, rich cloth caressed her skin, fine foods made her plump and happy. All her money is gone now, spent on doctors, physicians, surgeons, call them what you will – they could not heal her.

For twelve years they have dosed and robbed her.

Later in the sermon the woman makes a decision to go after Jesus:

Illness has folded her in on herself and shame has kept her indoors and she is weak and afraid. But the longing to be healed, to be touched, is still strong.

Head down and scarf covering her face she walks down towards the crowds who signal the arrival of this man. She must be careful because if she is noticed she will certainly be spat upon and maybe even stoned.

Until there. Suddenly he is there, back towards her.

All I need to do is to touch him.

He will never know, never know how I contaminated him, but he can, he will heal me.

Her hand reaches forward and she watches it, amazed. Fingers graze against cloth and there is a feeling of – power, through her and a sudden sense of wholeness.

He turns.

Who touched me?

Full of shame, twelve years of fear and shame and isolation, she feels the crowd go silent and slowly turn on her.

But his eyes looking for hers are not hostile. He reaches out, touches her face.

Daughter, your faith has made you well.

The miracle of healing, the wonder of love, the touch of a hand.

So simple, this happy ending.

So if you have been made to feel ashamed, this story is for you.

In Luke's gospel there is a story that explores a similar theme (Luke 7:36–50). Once again an unclean woman touches Jesus. Luke describes her as 'a woman who had lived a sinful life'. Whatever the nature of her sin the encounter with Jesus takes place at a meal in Simon the Pharisee's house. Among a group of males, religious, powerful and disapproving, the woman commits the utterly shocking act of letting down her hair. She weeps at Jesus' feet and begins to dry them with her hair, kissing them. In a gloriously extravagant gesture she pours expensive perfume over them.

The commentaries fill out the background. They point out that a woman would loose her hair only in the presence of her husband; that the Talmud taught that a breach of this custom constituted grounds for divorce; they observe that the perfume is probably a tool of her trade – to make her attractive to men; they comment on the taboo against touching and kissing a man's feet.

Even in our touchy-feely culture the scene is almost unbelievable. Imagine a diocesan synod interrupted by the entrance of a notorious call girl. She flings herself at the feet of a young priest, weeping passionately. Most of those watching draw their own conclusions and wait for the scandal to break in the newspapers. Later, of course, it is revealed that his pastoral care for the woman's little daughter has led her to rethink her life of prostitution. What went on in the synod was just an unusually uninhibited way of showing gratitude. Even so, not a few of those present think, 'Hmm'.

Why would we think that things would be so different in Jesus' day? What is astonishing about Jesus is the fact that in this exposed and embarrassing situation he does not reject the woman's touch. He doesn't flinch or gently turn away; there's no awkward cough or apologetic gesture to the host. Luke, the master storyteller, gives us a stage direction in verse 44: 'he turned towards the woman *and said to Simon* ...' Jesus speaks to Simon but the whole speech is spoken facing away from him and towards the woman. Her touch is accepted as the extravagant outpouring of a heart that has been touched by love. And he is deeply moved by her generosity and devotion, moved enough to gaze into her eyes and give her unstinting praise.

Lepers in the Soul

These stories are all about accepting those whom society rejects. They remind us of the power of touching and allowing ourselves to be touched. The actions of Jesus show that he will gladly violate and collude in the violation of his culture's taboos. He will not accept his society's estimate and treatment of the two women or the leper.

Unfortunately, we know that society's estimate very easily becomes our own. If father, mother and teacher tell a child that she is worthless and will come to no good, the prophecy fulfils itself. I remember talking to a young woman with a first class honours degree in mathematics. She was sure that she was hopeless at everything and would be incapable of finding a job. As we went on I realized that for most of her life she had been told she would come to nothing much. Some months later I met her parents. Five minutes with the mother showed me why her daughter spent her days in quiet despair.

Those who have been taught that they are rubbish learn to live in a deep pit with steep sides. Every attempt to climb out

is crushed. They are unclean, everything they touch is contaminated. Often the doctrines of the Christian faith push them
deeper into the mire. 'Miserable offenders', 'not worthy to
gather up the crumbs', total depravity, original sin – strong
words that may rightly call the complacent to repentance
serve only to bruise the wounded spirit.

In a blistering sermon Susan Durber lays out the sense of
pollution that accompanies feelings of self-dislike. She is
preaching on Ash Wednesday, that day in the Christian year
which reminds us that we are dust and that to dust we shall
return. But the sermon takes an unusual course. She accepts
that men and women are dust, but vehemently attacks the lie
that they are therefore rubbish, that the love of God shines more
radiantly the more they think of themselves as loathsome and
disgusting:

> Many of you experience the monthly shame which we are
> bidden to call a curse and to speak of only in whispers.
> Many of you will have strong and fleshly passions which
> have led you to shame and self-loathing. Many of us have
> learnt that we are rubbish, that we are dirt and shame and
> death – and that we are to be grateful to God for loving us
> despite ourselves – being weak and foolish and loathsome.[2]

She will not accept the lie and ends the sermon triumphantly:
'We are dust, always returning to the rich nobility of earth.
And we are a little lower than God, you and I, always returning
to the true and beautiful source of our being. The time is
fulfilled; repent and believe in the good news.'

Some find it hard to silence 'the lie' that demeans the
self; so many life experiences have reinforced the sense of self-
dislike. The voices of parents come back to haunt them: 'Such
a plain child. An awkward lumbering creature'; 'You naughty,
naughty boy. What a wicked thing to do'; 'Why can't you be

---

2 Susan Durber, 'Ash Wednesday', in Heather Walton and Susan Durber
(eds.), *Silence in Heaven*, London, SCM Press, 1994, pp. 51–4.

more like Stephanie?'; 'You'll never make anything of yourself'; 'You must do better than that if you're to please Daddy'; 'If you behave like that Mummy won't love you any more.' A deputy head of a large comprehensive school, apparently confident and assertive, suddenly had a total breakdown. She was the child of an Army family, her father a colonel. A colleague confided, 'I think she was always on parade.' Sometimes the root cause lies in past experiences bitterly regretted but unresolved: an abortion, being subjected to rape, an extramarital affair, being abused as a child, a shabby betrayal of a friend.

Self-loathing sometimes manifests itself in dramatic and bewildering forms. Until recently hurting oneself in the form of deliberate physical injury was largely unacknowledged. Those who suffered, suffered in solitary anguish. Even now when information about self-harm is more easily available it is often met with perplexity. Cutting, stabbing and scratching the skin, burning oneself, bruising the flesh, deliberately opening up sores, biting the inside of the mouth, resist explanation. Those who hear about these injuries are baffled and unable to get inside the mind of the perpetrator.

The reasons for self-harm are complex and no one explanation will cover all cases. In any case, respect for the person demands that their personal account be taken seriously. Nevertheless, it does seem as if much self-harm comes from anger directed against the self. The anger causes high levels of anxious tension that scream out for relief. These can be the result of trauma, guilt, or feelings of inadequacy and failure. Those who have been hurt can turn that hurt in on themselves, believing that they are 'bad' or 'dirty'.

Many of those who harm themselves find that others treat them with impatience or resentment. Even hospitals can be damaging places when someone is feeling vulnerable. But Sheena's story shows how touch can change even desperate situations:

There was this staff called Jean, she was all right, I could talk to her. Once when she was on nights I went to her and told her that I wanted to cut or burn myself. She asked me if she could touch my hand and my arm. I said yes and she just stroked me, calmly, up and down my hand and my arm, up and down. She talked to me. Told me to close my eyes and to imagine a chaotic place, bustling and full of people and noise and then she told me to think of walking away from there and described a walk that took me in my mind to a quiet peaceful place. I couldn't believe it, the need to cut went away.[3]

The parallels with the leper are notable. It was society that excluded the lepers, declared them dirty and denied them a voice. Jesus accepted and listened, and most significantly – given that so much self-harm involves breaking the skin – was not repulsed by the leper's skin.

I don't wish to suggest that solutions are easy to come by for anyone who believes they are unlovable and dirty. Nevertheless, the story of how Jesus cared for the leper has its own power and should not be dismissed. After all, this is the Jesus who was crucified outside the city walls because his death would contaminate the city and whose body was hastily taken down from the cross because it would pollute the sacred festival. The story of the leper can still speak to those who feel themselves to be lepers in the soul. Convinced that they are dirty and polluted, they are sure that they soil everything and everyone they touch. They are a hopeless case. The guilt and stain are too deeply ingrained for cleansing. They cannot manage even the leper's cry 'You can make me clean'. To all such people, I want to say, 'Please, hear the word of the Lord.' Jesus says to you, 'I will. Be clean.' Feel his touch on you. Feel his hands lifting you to your feet. Get off your knees knowing that he accepts you and makes you clean.

3 Gerrilyn Smith, Dee Cox and Jacqui Saradjin, *Women and Self-Harm*, London, The Women's Press, 1998, p. 52.

MAKING A COMEBACK

After he has healed the man, Jesus takes steps to restore him. It is strange to read the instructions to go to the priest and offer the sacrifices that Moses commanded. How odd that Jesus should be so careful about the conventions and the regulations when he has been so free with the boundaries and taboos.

In fact, with his realistic grasp of what life is like, Jesus appreciates that this man has got to begin to live in the normal world. That's why he says, 'Don't talk about it and get yourself noticed. Go and do everything that's right. Get your certificate of health and begin to live a new life in the community.' Jesus who breaks our conventions, knows that life has to be lived within those conventions. He may violate cultural norms but he knows we have to live in one culture or another. And he is concerned about that. It is as if he says, 'Let me get the man right for tomorrow, not just rejoicing in what's happened today.'

I think this is one more piece of evidence that Jesus is concerned that we should stand on our feet and enjoy a proper human independence. 'Worm theology' tells us that we are not much better than food for worms. It drives us back to wailing, gnashing of teeth and breast beating. Jesus echoes God's words to Ezekiel, 'Son of man, stand up on your feet ...' (Ezekiel 2:1). God has made us a little lower than the angels, and crowned us with those regal attributes, glory and honour. We are not rubbish. In a year or two this leper will be a pillar of his community, married with a young family, honoured in the gate of the city, with enough self-respect to cherish and affirm his wife and tell his children daily that they are the best thing since God invented manna.

So the man sets off with a light heart to see the priest, leaving the man who had restored him to return to the multitudes and his work of touching, healing, restoring those who were outside the safe circle. And now Jesus says to us, 'In my name and in my strength, go and do likewise.'

REFLECTION

'A hands-on God.' How can you be a hands-on person?

Reflect on times when you have lost a measure of your independence and have had to submit to being treated like an object, touched, handled – even manhandled. Has the example of Christ at his trial and mocking anything to say to those experiences?

Look at some hymns in your church hymn book. How do they explore images of cleansing and pollution.

'Touch is a sign of Christ's grace.' When has that been true for you?

DISCUSSION

Take a newspaper and go through it, stopping at each picture. Read what the journalist has written about the person(s) in the picture. Has the story drawn a boundary? If so, should a follower of Jesus try to cross that boundary? How?

Boundaries, classes, categories, groups and stereotypes are probably inevitable and often useful. When do they become damaging and what can we do about it?

'Holy people seem remarkably prone to catch whatever's going.' Discuss the relationship between holiness, purity and fear of defilement in the church. What do you understand by the term 'holiness'?

PRAYER

> Lord of wholeness and holiness,
> of the healing touch,
> and the betrayer's kiss,

You broke boundaries, give me your courage.
You defied convention, give me your freedom.
You touched untouchables, give me your love.

When I shrink from the touch of the unlovely,
bid me see them with your eyes.
When I can do nothing for myself,
bid me think on your helplessness.
When I am treated like an object,
bid me remember your wounds.

CHAPTER 5

THE FINGER OF GOD

A colleague got up from his chair in the staffroom and grinned amiably at me. 'Well, here we go,' he said. 'Last period Friday afternoon and 10Z! Say one for me with the big guy upstairs.' It was a joke, of course. No one would have been more surprised if a large fist had zapped a class of unruly wills and given him a quiet ending to the week.

But the remark made me think. The questions it raises are breathtaking. Does God *do* things in the world? And does he do them in response to my, or anybody else's, prayers? Do some people have a hotline to God so that they are worth having on your side? Why shouldn't my friend say one for himself? Does God jump to answer sudden prayers from distant acquaintances? Or does he play hard to get with those who have stood him up? Will God do things in response to prayer that he has no intention of doing otherwise? Do our prayers alter divine forward planning and performance targets?

Conversations about prayer and the power of God are like wandering over a minefield. For many, believers and unbelievers, prayer is a complete cop-out and talk of answered prayer just infuriates them. When your life is in ruins it is maddening to hear someone claiming that God found them a free parking place in the multi-storey. Great Aunt Maisie's toe would presumably have got better on its own without the massive storming of the citadels of heaven mounted by the Women's Bright Hour Intercessors' Circle. 'I'll pray for you' sounds like pious claptrap; a loan of £50 would be more useful. And, for the conscientious Christian struggling to persist in prayer and not to give up, there's always the uncomfortable adage 'If you want to shame Christians, ask them about their prayers.'

JESUS AND THE FINGER OF GOD:
THE POINT AT WHICH THINGS HAPPEN

One good place to begin is with an image used by Jesus in the middle of a controversy with his opponents: 'But if I drive out demons *by the finger of God*, then the kingdom of God has come to you' (Luke 11:20). The picture is a startling one: Jesus is the sharp end of God's activity in the world. It is worth exploring this image. If Jesus is the embodiment of God, *if God is Christlike*, then we may be able to read off from what Jesus did in his world something of the way God works in ours.

As soon as we look at the gospels we see a Jesus who is (literally) immersed in our world, down in the river with the rest of us, as he was at his baptism in the Jordan. Jesus gets his hands dirty. He does things, so that his followers will call him 'Jesus of Nazareth *mighty in deed and word*'. Wherever he is, things happen. This position is our base and whatever else we may want to say, we begin here. Jesus' words and deeds affirm that God is active in our world. He inserts himself into its life.

In the gospels we see a battle against the powers of evil and all that that phrase includes – disease, decay, death, slavery to destructive forces and situations, prejudice, hardness of heart. Jesus systematically wages war on everything that destroys, distorts, cramps and enslaves human life – everything that prevents people being what they were created to be. Wherever Jesus finds evil in his ministry he opposes it. The movement of his life, its driving force and direction, is *against* evil and *for* health, freedom, forgiveness, wholeness and fullness of life.

This is why Jesus' actions were called signs. 'If I by the finger of God cast out demons then know that the kingdom of God is come upon you.' Where God reigns evil is put to flight; if evil was being put to flight then God was at work. Fingers point and prod. The mighty works and words were like God's fingerprint, marks that he was present. What Jesus did and said pointed to the kingdom of God – that part of the cosmos where God is king and has his way. They were signs of a different and better world. He was constantly in the business of transformation. In Jesus we can see and feel the pull of this new world.

This aspect of Christ's character is instantly attractive to us. We need to hold on to it when the going gets rough and when we are tempted to give up praying. Put simply, Jesus is not removed, cold or dispassionate. He is no celestial bureaucrat, shuffling our application forms on his desk, clearing his throat and talking about 'giving it due attention with an answer next week or possibly at the end of the month'. He assures us that God will be equally energetic, involved and in the thick of the action.

WHAT ON EARTH IS GOD PLAYING AT? GOD'S SIGNATURE

I have called this image of Jesus, constantly at work for good and against evil, our base. It is the sign to which we must return. As we enter the thick undergrowth that obscures the pathways between divine power, human prayer and human need, we need to take the sign seriously. Heaven knows, there is enough nastiness in the world to call it into question. C. S. Lewis remarked, 'Every tombstone is a monument to unanswered prayer.' It is only human at times to complain, 'What on earth is God playing at?' When we feel that way we come back to the image of Jesus 'going about doing good'. He is like the 'ministry spokesperson' who tells you the Government's line on any issue. Jesus' actions make clear where God stands on the matter of evil. Do we believe him?

If we do, though difficulties do not evaporate, yet some of their sting is drawn. It becomes more difficult to say, 'What is God playing at? What does he think he's doing?' Of course, there will still be many occasions when we are bewildered and desolate and, in fact, the Bible sanctions our protests in those circumstances. But, in the light of Jesus' war on evil, we have to stop and think before accusing God of indifference or unjust dealing. The activity of Jesus contradicts many of the well-meaning but hurtful things people say when trouble strikes. It cannot ever be right to say, 'God creates cancer', and it is certainly wrong to say, 'It was the will of God that our child got leukaemia.' Jesus waged war on everything that destroyed, distorted, cramped and enslaved human life.

Questions remain, of course, many of them very painful ones: 'Why does he not overthrow evil in this dramatic way today?', 'Why does nothing happen when I pray?', 'Why are some healed and others not?', 'Why do Christians so often run for cover into a shelter they call Mystery and I call Cop-out?'

THE COSMIC WAITER: ANYTHING YOU ASK FOR

Christians have always connected God's power with prayer but the questions listed in the preceding paragraph suggest that this can be done in too crude, immediate and physical a manner. Prayer does connect with God's activity but the works of God might not be primarily about restoring people to health. After all, everyone whom Jesus raised from the dead died later on – Lazarus, Jairus' daughter, the widow of Nain's son. We live in a decaying and dying world. Jesus appeared not to arrest its progress permanently, at least not in the time of his ministry.

'Say one for me' often sounds like the words of someone who wants a quick fix. 'Say one for me' wants the goodies but without any time-consuming and health-endangering involvement with the God who makes it happen. It's easy to relate to God as if he were the heavenly Cash Dispenser. We insert the card, key in the right PIN number, press all the buttons and when the £20 notes fail to appear we kick the machine. This assumes that God's activity is entirely devoted to our happiness *as we define it*. We want him to act now to give us what we perceive as good for us.

In a memorable scene from *Fawlty Towers*, Basil Fawlty starts to lash his car with a handy branch because 'it refuses to start'. 'Right', he screams. 'You've asked for it!' We know that cars can't think, feel, withhold their consent or ask for anything, but I'm not sitting in judgement on Basil Fawlty – I've spat at my computer too many times. Sometimes we behave as if prayer is like that: I followed the procedure and got the message 'System Error'. What do I do now? Count to ten and pray again?

This view of prayer has been termed 'God as cosmic waiter'. We enter the celestial restaurant and expect to be presented with the menu. We choose dishes that tickle our fancy and give the order to a waiter who is shimmying around, deferentially devoted to our every whim. The wine list arrives and we select a little something suited to our palate and pocket. We expect to get what we ordered and we do expect the service to be prompt. If there's a fly in the soup we complain. If the service is speedy then the waiter may get a tip; if it is long delayed we shall gripe and ask what he thinks he is playing at. I know that in our heads we don't think prayer is like that, but in the place where feelings lurk, it's different.

We can find the cosmic waiter model of prayer in the gospels. The religious authorities ask for a sign (Matthew 12:38), the crowds follow Jesus in the hope of another free feed (John 6:26), the mother of James and John prays on behalf of her sons (Matthew 20:20). Her prayer is classic: 'Please can my boys sit on Jesus' right hand and his left in glory.' But what would have happened if Jesus had granted the prayer? It's a crass, wrong-headed request coming from a wrong motive, and it spells disaster.

Jesus was wise not to grant these prayers. We can readily grant that not every request is in our best interests. Billy Graham's wife says that if God had granted every prayer she prayed she would have married the wrong man – several times. In the legend of Dr Faustus, Faustus strikes a deal with the devil. He gets everything his heart desires but in the process loses the centre of his life – his soul. The myth of Midas tells of a king who is given the gift of turning everything he touches into gold – a wonderful example of a prayer answered – but destroys his daughter when his lips touch her in a goodnight kiss.

We may think these examples are one-sided. Not every prayer is utterly selfish. What if I pray that I may win the lottery, thinking, no doubt of all the good I could do and all the happiness I could spread around – with a modest amount of both for myself? It's not the most disinterested prayer but it would surely increase the sum of human happiness, particularly if I promise to spend most of the money on medical research and not on fast cars and swimming pools. But this example provokes a more fundamental question than 'Can I wheedle my way round God?' What if this talk of orders to waiters and cash dispensers is a blind alley? What if God is not mainly interested in my short-term happiness but interested to the point of obsession with bringing me into bliss?

If this is so then time and again God must be frustrated by our prayers. One of the saddest stories in the gospels is that of the ten lepers who were healed by Jesus (Luke 17:17). Nine of them went gaily on their way, thoroughly satisfied with health and happiness. They had put in their application and, lo, it had been granted within minutes. That's what they'd come for and that's what they got. Now it was time for a celebration. Only one turned his face back towards the person who had healed him. But in turning back to look at the face of Christ, he opened himself up to the possibility of a gift that might be more than skin-deep. Luther said, 'We ask for silver and God longs to give us gold.' And, to be honest, often we ask for dross.

God's Deeper Work: Coaxing us into Life

'Finger of God' is an evocative image. It reminds me of the Michelangelo fresco on the ceiling of the Sistine Chapel. The painting shows God's finger stretched out towards Adam. Within the next second life and power will be transmitted from finger tip to finger tip. We wait for the spark to leap across the gap. We know that this means the creation of Adam, the moment when the life of the spirit enters his body. After this contact he will no longer be a clod of earth, or dust, or animal, but a living soul. One critic observes that what is often missed by the viewer is the look of *longing* on the face of Adam. This moment is the moment he becomes all he was designed to be.

What is God doing in this painting? It is an icon of what I have called his deeper work. To create something is to love it. And to love it means constantly to try to coax it into life. The works of Jesus show us that God loves this world and will do anything to win it back. Jesus' miracles are little vignettes of God restoring the beauty and purity of humanity and of the created world. He rebukes demons, disease and the storm. Legion is left seated, clothed and in his right mind. God's project is to win everyone and everything to himself by means of love. The ultimate fact of the universe is the love of God constantly reaching out to us.

Our perspective on prayer begins to shift when we once suppose that God has a deeper work in mind than ticking off the items on our shopping list like a helpful assistant in ASDA.

Imagine a couple who have been invited out to dinner. On the surface the evening is everything you could wish for – the table laid with the best cutlery and silver candlesticks, soft music playing in the background, the food beautifully cooked, the wines superb. Each course is served elegantly and without delay; the host and hostess are attentive, assiduously watchful of their guests. But in the car going home, the man turns to his wife and says, 'Enjoy it?' 'Ye-es, I suppose so. But I don't feel we know them any better now than we did before.' 'Mmm,' he replies. 'You know, I don't think they realized that feeding us wasn't the point of the evening.'

Most meals with friends are not about solving the problem of nutrition. We can eat perfectly well at home. The meal is the opportunity to work through a different agenda – that of getting to know one another, sharing something of ourselves, deepening a friendship.

That is God's project as well. God is desperate to find creatures who will freely open themselves up to his love and power, who will allow themselves to be drawn into the divine purposes and to know his love more intimately. God looks for a relationship of love with us. He delights in us. There is a deep maternal instinct in him. Sadly, he is often frustrated.

He also wants us to delight in him, because we are fulfilled when we find our rest and life and joy in him. Then at last everything is working properly and we discover our reason for being. Until that happens our lives are spinning, looking for a still point. Worship is not God finally getting us to compliment him for eternity as if he were infinite vanity. Worship is us dancing in delight in the dance of the universe; it's us singing with everything that has breath in one unbroken harmony when we join the music of the spheres. And prayer is the heart of worship.

There is a wonderful story in Thomas Merton's anthology of stories of the Desert Fathers that points us to God's deeper agenda:

> Abbot Lot came to Abbot Joseph and said: 'Father, according as I am able, I keep my little rule, and my little fast, my prayer, meditation and contemplative silence; and according as I am able I strive to cleanse my heart of thoughts: now what more should I do?' The elder rose up in reply and stretched out his hands to heaven, and his fingers became like ten lamps of fire. He said, 'Why not be totally changed into fire?'[1]

Relationships are deepened in ways other than quiet chats in peaceful places. The story of the Syro-Phoenician woman (Mark 7:26) thrusts us almost roughly into a different world. She comes to Jesus in distress, crying on behalf of her daughter, 'Drive the demon out of my daughter'. This is not a plea for gratification of a whim. She receives an answer that stuns us by its savagery: 'It is not right to take the children's bread and give it to dogs.' Can this be Jesus speaking? A mother beside herself with anxiety is compared to the dogs

---

1 Thomas Merton, *The Wisdom of the Desert*, London, Sheldon Press, 1974, p. 50.

scavenging under the dinner table? Immediately she rejoins, 'Yes, Lord. But even the dogs under the table eat the children's crumbs.'

Mark makes no comment on the subtext; we have to make the best of the interchange for ourselves and I realize that there is more than one way of taking the passage. What is certain is that a prayer is brutally rebuffed and Jesus appears to turn his back on the woman's distress. But prayer refuses to be silent; it continues to cry out and breaks through to a more profound place of meeting. We are not told about Jesus' thoughts here but I speculate that his reaction to her riposte is 'Yes! That's what I wanted more than anything else. I was hoping that you would come back at me.' The woman goes beyond politeness. This is a vigorous and robust engagement with God, honest, naked, desperate, beyond piety and platitudes. Put off, she springs back. It is a parable of wrestling with God in prayer and, somehow, finding him in the struggle.

Praying is not usually so agonized. Indeed, more often than not it is routine and mundane, bringing the details of our lives to God in a daily round-up of the news. What place does this style of praying have in God's deeper work? It's helpful to see it, in Karl Barth's phrase, as 'making room for God'. Just as our human friendships deepen through inconsequential sharing of hopes and fears, so our friendship with God is nourished by conversation. In this transaction *the detail* of our prayers plays a vital role. In his letter to the Philippian church Paul urges his readers to talk to God about everything: 'Do not be anxious about anything, but in everything, by prayer and petition, with thanksgiving, present your requests to God. And the peace of God, which transcends all understanding, will guard your hearts and your minds in Christ Jesus' (Philippians 4:6,7).

Talk to God about everything, by which the apostle presumably means everything – big, small, silly, life-changing. Are you scared to drive into London, anxious about a lump on your body, not sure whether someone snubbed you this morning, bothered about having a pimple on your nose, uncertain how you are going to manage financially, in a sweat about the meeting on Thursday, worried that you can't sleep, not coping with work or study, terrified by X, where X stands for teacher, boss, client, group? Paul's response is 'talk to God about everything. Thank him where you can. Ask him for things.' You may not get the answer in the form you want it but go on talking to him.

I find it significant that Jesus seldom tells us why we should pray; he just says, 'Don't give up or lose heart. Go on doing it.' But isn't that the way every friendship works?

Contracted to a Span:
The Word Written on Flesh

God's longing for us may be the most important thing about prayer, but we may still feel that many questions are unanswered. We still want to know if prayer changes things and is not just part of personal therapy. Jesus assures the disciples that whatever they ask *in his name*, the Father will readily grant. The trouble is that his promises seem not to match the actual experience of praying. Many, perhaps most, petitions are not answered in the way Jesus outlined. The problem is partly that the offer is set in such expansive terms: 'Whatever you ask ...' Not 'quite a lot of what you ask ...' or 'from time to time, if you're lucky ...' Ironically, we would probably settle for the less comprehensive deal. But 'whatever' leaves little margin for error on God's part. Two thousand years of Christian spirituality have consistently affirmed that prayer is connected to the action of God in the world. 'Say one for me' implies that somehow prayer releases the activity of God, though it is not a matter of overcoming his reluctance so much as taking hold of his willingness. Either Jesus was misleading his disciples or he has got the whole business of prayer wrong – desperate conclusions for us to draw – or we have not properly understood the condition, 'in my name'.

I return to the starting point of the chapter. The gospels describe the deeds of Jesus as works of power in that that divine power was let loose through him. He was the point of contact. Power was funnelled through him and exploded into our world, leaping as a spark arcs across the gap in a car engine. In a strange phrase Jesus declared that he felt it going out of him like a physical surge. He sensed it when he healed a woman with a perpetual haemorrhage (Mark 5:25). In Jesus the chasm between earth and heaven was bridged, contact was established between the world of eternity and the world of flesh and matter.

A number of images spring to mind. Even though all analogies are misleading in one way or another, they may help us see a little of how divine power was let loose in Jesus. For example, we can picture Jesus as the perfect translator, authentically and accurately translating the speech of heaven into a language we can understand. Or Jesus is the perfect dancer, embodying in physical action every gesture and movement that lives in the imagination of the divine choreographer. Or he is the perfect channel for the torrent of the divine life, with no boulder or blockage in the way of its free flowing. Or he is the lightning conductor, the contact point that allows all 100 million volts of divine energy to burst into our world. However inadequate these analogies, they focus on the perfect harmony between Father and Son. Now we can see what is meant by doing something 'in the name'. If a new and living way has been established between Spirit and flesh, then no wonder things happen through Jesus; no wonder he raises the dead and drives out demons; no wonder they convulse, squirm and writhe, like slugs on salt.

The prayer of Jesus in Gethsemane takes us to the heart of what it means to keep in touch with God. We stand on holy ground. Jesus prays in agony, 'Father, if you are willing, take this cup from me; yet not my will, but yours be done' (Luke 22:42). We see the heart of prayer. In Mark's version, Jesus says, 'everything is possible for you' (Mark 14:36). It is a misreading of the dynamics of the passage to suppose that Jesus is either blind or reluctant as he prays. The words are words of faith, trust and obedience. He shrinks from the appalling pain that lies ahead, but he knows that the cross is the only way in which the world can be redeemed. All other ways involve God in being false to himself. God may crush all freedom and force compliance and obedience out of people; God may act as celestial steamroller but the price is unthinkable. 'Not my will but yours be done.' And there the prayer finds its home. From a distance we who know something of the story can see from that alignment of wills that there followed the explosions of power into the world that we call Good Friday, Easter Day and Pentecost.

GOD'S FINGERTIP: TRYING TO GET STRUCK BY LIGHTNING

I've tried to show that asking 'in the name' is about contact between wills and is more than a verbal formula. The fingers of God and Adam in the Michelangelo painting remind me of a trust game sometimes played during weekend conferences on relationships. One person is blindfolded and is led around by a partner purely through the contact of finger tip to finger tip. To take part in such an activity teaches you a lot about trust, concentration – and fear. In many ways it is like prayer. When you do it right, trust grows and the emotional bond between the couple deepens. But the physical link – finger tip to finger tip – is a terribly fragile one and is easily broken. Hasty movements, a moment of self-assertion, a lapse of concentration and the blindfolded partner can break the connection and be left feeling desolate. The power and freedom of the seeing partner can be communicated to the one who cannot see, but not on demand. It is offered as a gift and needs to be received as such. And for both partners the activity will take all their concentration and effort. Sometimes I come to prayer and feel as if I am standing in the dark with my finger stuck up in the air waiting to feel the touch of God's finger on mine. And it often seems as if the main thing he wants to say to me is 'Stop waving your hand about. If you'd keep still I could make

contact.' The old saying *laborare est orare* is usually translated 'to work is to pray'; it ought to mean that praying is very
hard work.

The blindfolded partner is foolish to think that he or she can
find the way without help. Perhaps this is why the gospels
present us with so many examples of prayer that releases the
power of God, but only when it is spoken in weakness. A
woman, feeling herself polluted, creeps hesitantly through the
crowd to touch the hem of Jesus' garment, risking discovery
and contempt (Matthew 9:20). A father driven out of his mind
calls out to Jesus, 'I do believe. Help me where my faith falls
short' (Mark 9:24). And their prayers are answered. Jesus' question to the disciples just before the feeding of the five thousand, 'Where shall we buy bread for these people to eat?' (John
6:5), seems designed to highlight the enormous gap between
the demands being made on them and *the resources* they have
to meet those demands. He presses their faces up against the
problem: 'Without me, you don't have very much.'

I remember someone talking to me about a time when she
had been appointed to a senior post in education. Eighteen
months in she had reached the end of her resources. 'Lord, I
can't manage,' she prayed. She told me that it was as if she
heard Christ reply, 'I have been waiting for you to realize that
you couldn't manage on your own.' The cry from the bottom of
the pit is what Christ is hoping for. He says to us, 'I want you
to feel like the friend at midnight. A visitor comes late at night
– at an inconvenient hour, when you are unprepared. The rules
of hospitality demand that you feed him – and you have
nothing. There is nothing else you can do but go in great
distress to your nearest friend and begin to beat upon the
door.' Sometimes Christ says to us, 'How long before you
realize you must beat upon the door? I want you to understand
that, like branches detached from the vine, without me you
can do nothing.'

On my last visit to the Holy Land I visited an orphanage
in Bethany. A mother and daughter run it. They have a policy
never to turn any child away, so they take children when there

seems to be no room, beyond what is humanly possible. Once they found three children abandoned in a chicken coop, a two-year-old girl, her sister aged seven and a boy of four. The youngest girl's skin was eaten into by worms. They took them in and looked after them with such care that, a year later, visiting social aid workers asked, 'Have you changed her skin?' But their reply was 'Love works a miracle.' I was reminded of the perfume Mary poured over Jesus' feet – and the fragrance filled the house. Here are women who daily confront problems that are beyond them, but find that in their weakness is God's strength. I felt as if I was looking at the face of Christ in those women. They make contact with him and unbelievable things happen.

An Untidy Business: A God who Chooses to Work with Amateurs

God must find waiting for us to pray a frustrating business, especially since he seems to want us to work with him of our own free will. Sometimes people talk about prayer in terms of a masterscript that God follows to the letter. Unanswered prayer is explained by saying, 'It wasn't the will of God.' The problem with this kind of talk is that it can suggest that the will of God is some sort of juggernaut: you'd better climb on board or it will crush you.

In *Love for the Lost*, a novel by Catherine Fox, Adam and Isobel discuss the idea of a divine masterscript:

'There is a script, but it's improvised.'

Controlled by the actors, not the playwright, you mean?

'Apparently. But supposing, in spite of everything, the playwright can hold it all in his mind – all the characters, the plots and endless chaotic sub-plots, the red herrings, the cock-ups, the disastrous death of the hero – and weave all the strands together? I picture the action as being brooded over by a keen, but infinitely kind, intelligence and he will bring it all to its fitting conclusion.'

She was moved. So he was capable of laying aside his endless clever games and being sincere. Did it feel like intellectual nakedness to him, after all this time?

If the conclusion is inevitable, why bother? she asked. *What does our puny contribution mean?*

'Everything and nothing. God doesn't need us, but He's chosen to work with amateurs.'[2]

This way of looking at life is both exciting and daunting. It also makes our response to God vastly important. Because if he chooses to work with us, then the unwillingness to open oneself to Christ may close down the possibility of a relationship and frustrate his purpose. Jesus goes to Nazareth and they cannot see anything special in him. They know him too well. The gospel records, 'He could not do any miracles there ... And he was amazed at their lack of faith' (Mark 6:5,6). It is true that Mark adds that 'he healed a few sick people' but when the shutters come down even divine love and power has a job to do much. Already the good residents of Nazareth are on the long journey to shutting themselves up totally within themselves. There is a self-absorption that is hell, because there is no chink, no tiny crack through which the love and life of God can come.

The last paragraph may be misleading. What can we say about those situations where we pray for two people to recover from similar illnesses and find that one gets better and the other dies. Indeed, someone has said that the real problem is not unanswered but *answered* prayer. I have suggested that Jesus was unable to do any mighty work in Nazareth because

2 Catherine Fox, *Love for the Lost*, London, Penguin Books, 2000, p. 342.

of their unbelief. Did those who prayed for the person who died lack faith? Or did they not make contact in the right way? Were they not distressed enough? Or show enough weakness?

Even to say these things is grossly insulting to all who have prayed at their wits' end for those they love. Prayer is not a knack. I want to reaffirm that our openness to God is a key factor. But other factors are present in every situation as well. In the next chapter I shall argue that God respects his creation and gives it a measure of freedom. The freedom that is given to human beings is given in a comparable way to every element in creation – even down to genes, viruses and cells. This means that every situation has its own indeterminacy, its own constraints and inbuilt limits. These are vastly complicated and far beyond our capacity to identify. What this amounts to is that two situations can be superficially the same but totally different in their deep structure. At the risk of being misunderstood, let me say boldly that God has space to work in one situation in a way that he does not have in the other. Our prayers are part of what gives him space. But our prayers alone do not define his room for manoeuvre.

This is not to imply that God can do nothing in the other case. The Lord's prayer teaches us that he is our father. Our father will do all that he can do in the specific situation. He will not play tricks on us. If we ask him for bread, he will not give us a stone; if we ask for a fish we won't be given a snake. This means that there is no such thing as unanswered prayer; God does something with every prayer. That is why we ought to keep on praying and never lose heart. But, equally, we must pray with our minds. John Pritchard comments on the need to frame our prayers with a view to the realities of the world, 'If I am a nurse and I hear simplistic prayers that so-and-so will be physically healed when I know full well that under normal conditions so-and-so has terminal cancer, then I am being asked to leave my mind at home.'[3] This is not to say that

3 John Pritchard, *The Intercessions Handbook*, London, SPCK, 1997, p. 3.

miracles do not happen. But in the end we rest on the faithfulness and love of God, who knows what he is doing and knows what is possible.

I remember seeing a television documentary on a mother with a child who was autistic and at times virtually uncontrollable. It seemed to me like a parable of the love of God for all his creation. I found it a profoundly moving experience to watch as she tried, with infinite care and patience, to find a way past the barricades, through to the child. Her efforts were frustrated again and again, often to the accompaniment of physical assault and no doubt much inner pain. Yet the most impressive aspect of the relationship was the mother's persistence, coupled with her refusal to react violently to the child. Her care was the opposite of vague sentimentality. Most of the time she was following strategies suggested to her by medical advisers. But this deliberate, thoughtful compassion was dominated by a desire to love the child into life.

Prayer is the way in which we open ourselves to God's love and connect with his power. It takes time and the 'effort' to be still. It requires the willingness to put the noisy mind to silence, to listen and wait on God. For prayer makes demands first on our character. As Augustine put it, 'prayer is taking the chalice to the fountain to be filled.' It is the forming of a heart that wants to be with Christ in his work of love and wants to know that love more than anything else, more even than seeing wonderful answers to prayer! For perhaps God is less interested in our triumphs and successes in the Christian life than in the depth of our friendship with him. This is his deep work in us. For all we know it may be the mightiest of his mighty works.

REFLECTION

Celestial bureaucrat, cosmic waiter, cash dispenser – in what ways are these images of the God to whom we pray inadequate? What image of God do you work with in your prayers?

Touching God's finger, beating on a door at midnight, taking
the chalice to the fountain to be filled – how do you picture
your experience of praying?

'Why not be totally changed into fire?' If Abbot Joseph had
said this to you, what would you want to say in reply?

Reflect on your experience of praying in times of personal
weakness.

'Whatever you ask in my name ...' What *practical* difference
does this make to the way we pray?

A Prayer Exercise

In your imagination hold your finger up before you, as a sign
that you are open to God's touch. Pray, 'Touch me with your
love, O Lord.' Talk to God about your life – what is big, small,
silly, life-changing. Pray again, 'Touch me with your love, O
Lord,' and wait quietly for the peace of God, which guards your
heart and mind.

Now think about something that prevents people (or a
particular person) being what they were meant to be: 'disease,
decay, death, slavery to destructive forces'. As a sign of God's
power over evil in your imagination point your finger at the
problem and pray, 'Touch them with your love, O Lord.'

A Prayer Sequence

This prayer is made up of sentence prayers from the gospels

It would be best to pray it slowly with pauses for reflection
between each sentence.

Lord, teach me to pray.
Sir, I have no one to help me.
Lord Jesus Christ, Son of the living God, have mercy on me.

Lord, I want to see.
Sir, give me this water.
Lord, come and see.
Nevertheless, not my will but yours be done.

Lord, you know all things; you know that I love you.
Only say the word and I shall be healed.

CHAPTER 6

THE WOUNDED HEALER

All the ultimate questions of human existence are raised in television soaps and series. That's probably why we continue to tune in. I remember a particularly disturbing episode of *Casualty*, the Accident and Emergency drama. A patient had been admitted in some pain with an illness later revealed to be AIDS. He also had earache. One of the nurses, trying to keep him in the picture said, 'It looks as though you may have a fungal infection of the ear.' He replied, 'I'm afraid.' 'What are you afraid of?' she asked. He said, 'I don't want to meet God. I am afraid to meet someone who gives me AIDS and throws in a fungal infection of the ear.'

We don't need to go to the television to find examples of pain. Our own pain raises all the problems we could ask for. In many ways, however, the pain of those we love is worse. Why should they have to endure it? A cleaner working in an old people's home says to me in great distress, 'Why does he put these old ladies on the earth only to reduce them to sticks and bones at the end?' A ninety-year-old woman, unable to get out of her flat, falls and breaks her arm in two places. She asks, plaintively, 'If only I knew what I'd done to deserve this, I could stand it.' We read about the last days of Iris Murdoch and grieve at the deterioration of what was one of the sharpest intellects of recent times. How could the pattern of her awesome mind be so scrambled and jumbled at the end?

Why is there pain? Perhaps that's not quite the question that hurts; let's rephrase it as 'Why is there such an *excess* of pain?' It's the excess of pain that is without meaning. Traditional answers – to punish, reform, purify, warn – will not fit. Indeed they are monstrously insulting to those who suffer. God as cosmic sadist is a more intelligible explanation. Why is the *timing* of pain often so perverse, coming when

91

things are at their worst or just at the threshold of a better phase of life? Why are the recipients so randomly and *undeservingly* selected? The pain of children, even the pain of animals, is especially hard to bear, because they are so pathetically innocent and vulnerable. And, behind all these questions, why, despite much prayer, does pain persist? Where is God when it hurts? At one time or another, most of us have sympathized with Ivan in *The Brothers Karamazov*: 'We cannot afford to pay so much for admission. And therefore, I hasten to return my ticket of admission. I accept God ... but I cannot accept the world that he has made.'

WHERE IS GOD WHEN IT HURTS?

There are no easy answers. We all have to handle the mess that comes at us in our own way. Yet at the centre of Christianity is a God crucified. The cross is a familiar symbol. We need to stand back from it a little to feel the paradox. It is such a shocking image that it ought to jolt us into asking, 'What can it mean? Why on earth would Christians want to put it on top of churches?' I remember a conversation with a woman who had a severely handicapped teenage son. For 17 years she had abused God. She said to me, 'If there's anyone up there at all, he's a devil.' At some point in the conversation, I said, 'The cross is the symbol of Christianity. That's why there are crosses everywhere in churches.' She suddenly leaned forward and said, not angrily this time but with urgency, 'Do you honestly believe that can help me?' Since pain is felt in our flesh, there is something fitting about putting the question 'Where is God when it hurts?' to the Jesus who came to us in the flesh.

I need to begin a little further back, however. The first reply to 'Where is God when it hurts?' has to be 'Sustaining the whole system.' This is a necessary beginning. God holds everything in his hands. He speaks the universe into existence and then keeps it going. The picture of a loom comes to mind.

The loom is constructed of a framework on which are attached vertical threads. On those vertical threads the tapestry will be woven. There is no predetermined pattern or colour for the tapestry and on one set of vertical threads an infinite variety of patterns could be woven. But whatever the finished work looks like, it will depend ultimately on the framework of the loom. If the framework were damaged or some of the warp threads cut, then the tapestry would collapse. In that sense everything that is woven will owe its existence to the loom. We cannot delete the influence of the loom from the finished work and in a similar way, we cannot detach God from everything that happens in his universe. The Ivan of Dostoevsky's novel may still want to return his ticket. But if he does, he won't get a God-free universe – he won't get a universe at all.

THE GROANS OF CREATION

Even if we grant that everything in an ultimate sense depends on God, it still makes sense to ask how he is implicated when · things go wrong now. Once again we demand, and more urgently this time, 'Where is God when it hurts?' I offer three possibilities, all of which are involved in any given situation.

First, the world is in the grip of the powers of evil. There are a number of points in the gospels where Jesus seems to assume this. For example, I'm not sure the devil was lying when he offered Jesus the kingdoms of this world. Jesus rejects the temptation but does not deny Satan's ability to make the offer. Apparently, Satan does have power in the world. The first letter of John states baldly, 'the whole world is under the control of the evil one' (1 John 5:19). Jesus presupposes this when he describes a crippled woman as 'this woman, a daughter of Abraham, whom Satan has kept bound for eighteen long years' (Luke 13:16). At his arrest he says, 'this is your hour – when darkness reigns' (Luke 22:53). Satan is the rapacious householder who keeps everything he has plundered shut up under lock and key. He will not willingly allow his domain to be ransacked. In fact, his booty will stay locked away until someone much stronger comes and overpowers him (Mark 3:27). In the parable of the sower, the evil one comes and snatches away the word (Mark 4:15). He sows tares in the field along with God's wheat (Matthew 13:25–8).

What do these pictures amount to? Even when every allowance has been made for metaphor, they suggest that Evil has a real, even if limited, power within the world. The first volume of C. S. Lewis's science fiction trilogy referred to earth as the silent planet, out of communication with God, dark and inhospitable, shut off.

Secondly, creation is fallen and flawed. We live in a universe that is running down. The world is decaying and has the smell of death about it. A fracture runs through the whole universe, like a split in a length of wood. In computer terms, there is a glitch in the deep structure of the software, which means that as the programme runs flaws and faults appear. Such a picture has come to mean more since the appearance of the computer virus Melissa. As hundreds, possibly thousands, of computers crashed, as hard disks were corrupted and the databases of national charities were wiped clean, we began to appreciate what a malign intelligence can do when it gets into the insides of the system. Melissa was a ghastly update of the parable of the wheat and the weeds. Even nastier was the 'I love you' virus because it found a toehold in our humanity, namely, our natural curiosity and the desire to be liked. So the garden of Eden came to Microsoft. In a vivid phrase St Paul says the creation groans like a wounded animal. It is an odd thing to say that this world is in pain, but many environmentalists use similar language. Flawed, fallen and fractured, inanimate and animate creation alike, at times it looks as if the whole thing is out of control. I remember how depressed I felt when I first read that dinosaurs suffered from arthritis! Of course, the image of a whimpering animal is not Paul's last word. In the same passage he talks as if creation is in its birth pangs; the pain of labour does look forward to birth. Meanwhile, however, nature and humanity groan. Our teeth decay and the liver fluke continues to feed off the insides of sheep.

Thirdly, God is responsible for making this world but he has set within it a degree of freedom, a measure of independence and autonomy. Thus he not only makes the world but makes it so that it can be itself by itself. We tend not to notice creation's freedom. What we notice is its regularity. It appears to work according to regular principles except for one interesting fact: no one can precisely predict what will come out. Freedom, flexibility, uncertainty and indeterminacy are at the centre of every tiny part of creation. At the macro level, creation's regularity is bound to be more visible than its freedom, just as my family only notice what they call my boring habits, foibles, routines and quirks. But at a level deeper than they observe I know that my routines are made up of thousands of infinitesimal choices. My predictable pattern of behaviour on Monday is not exactly the same as its repetition on Tuesday. In fact, I have freedom to change, even if only in a small way. I am not 100 per cent cause and effect, locked into a robot-like mechanical existence. (Were it not such an exhausting business, I expect I could manage a complete metamorphosis.) In a similar fashion the created universe appears to work according to regular principles that may be, if only we were able to observe what was really going on, more open and indeterminate than we think. It is encouraging to be told by scientist colleagues that both quantum theory and chaos theory hint at unpredictability at the heart of every bit of creation.

Why should God make such a universe? He gives it freedom because love is about letting be. Dante spoke of the love that moves the sun and the other stars. The love of God creates and lets what it creates be itself. Even though God sustains the universe he is not constantly overruling its behaviour. Indeed, if he overruled at every point, the universe would be a solid block, so to speak; it would have no gaps between the moving parts. The human spine is capable of movement because each vertebra possesses its own range of movement. Without the gaps it would be fused into an immovable single bone. As it is, though it cannot bend in absolutely any direction or to any degree, yet, within its limits, it is capable of a variety of movement and surprising flexibility. We might say that in a comparable way God's respect for his creation demands that he limit his total control and allow flexibility.

As these three suggestions jostle one another we may catch a glimpse of how we can live in a world with so much pain and suffering and evil. If there is anything in them, then it is wrong to say, 'God creates cancer'. In an episode of *Peak Practice* there was a scene where a nun was receiving chemotherapy for cancer. She looked at the cocktail of chemicals and said, 'I wonder if there is anything of God in these chemicals.' The doctor replied, 'Fight fire with fire. There's certainly nothing of God in the cancer.' We are and we live among systems of increasing complexity, all functioning and at times malfunctioning, unpredictable at the micro level, interacting with all other systems. Within such an almost infinite variety of possibilities you are bound to get grotesque parodies, nightmare variations on the theme of life. Genetic unravelling produces strange and terrible distortions of the code millions of branches down the line. Viruses flourish, finding purchase in this combination of cells but resisted in this. And so, somewhere in my genes, planted there by a grandparent 25,000 generations back, working through the millions of permutations and branching options in the millions of descendants of those original ancestors a cancerous possibility becomes a reality as it erupts in my body. Who is to blame? Does God cause these things? Only in the sense that he holds the loom together. The cancerous cells weave their own pattern across the threads but God keeps it all in place just as he keeps every planet and galaxy, every brain and heart, every molecule and gene in place. Just as he sustains the vocal chords of the man who says, 'There is no God'.

THE INEXHAUSTIBLE GOD

In the light of all this, how are we now to answer the question 'Where is God when it hurts?' Paul says, 'God is at work for good in everything.' We are invited to see this as the truth about every situation. God is working within it *for good*. But, given what I have written in the preceding paragraphs, perhaps we ought to express it as: God is working incessantly for good *within the space he's got*. We have already noted that God has set himself limits beyond which he will not go. There's a story that's been around a long time about a village where parents and children weave carpets together. The children make mistakes – fairly frequently – as children will. However, instead of undoing the mistakes their children make, the parents weave their own patterns around them. I don't think it matters much that this village has been variously located in Turkey, Lebanon and China! It will serve as a parable of the way God acts. God is at work in every situation for good – within the room available.

I cannot stress this enough. I like the picture of God as musician, the supreme improviser, who is constantly revising the melody and the harmony to take account of the discords coming at him from the rest of the band. Someone has said, 'God is always in the position of saying, "What to do now?"' Can we glimpse in this picture anything of the sheer audacity and genius of God, what the Jews might call his bare-faced *chutzpah*? I can understand why Clark Pinnock has said, 'God is not omnipotent but he is omnicompetent.' Some may hesitate at the thought that God is not omnipotent. Peter Baelz has expressed the same idea as 'God is doing all that love can do.'

From this viewpoint God's will is always being done on earth as in heaven, but we need to be careful about the way we speak of it. Bishop John Taylor says, 'The truth about God is not so much that he is omnipotent as that he is inexhaustible.' Imagine a mountain stream. Its course is always downhill and we know that it will get to the sea. At the same time we would be surprised if its course ran straight and unhindered. Rocks and boulders get in the way. A ridge runs across the direction of flow. Small stones dam the current so that it seems to stop. But patiently and persistently it searches for a way round, through, over or under. Nothing could be easier to divert or dam. At the same time, paradoxically, nothing is more unstoppable. Here is an image of the loving action of God. He is at work in every situation for good. And in the long term, probably the very long term, his love will triumph. All things are possible. But sometimes we need to say, 'No, it can't be done this way. Not even by God.'

From time to time we recognize his work and call it healing. Occasionally it is so unexpected that we call it miracle. But he is always at work for good within every situation – within the space that he's got for manoeuvre. This is why it is always worth praying, because prayer is opening ourselves up to God – and, to put it in an odd way, increasing his space. In the preceding chapter I suggested that Nazareth was an example of God hemmed in. 'He could not do any miracles there ... And he was amazed at their lack of faith' (Mark 6:5,6). Even the divine love and power found the space too cramped to do all that he longed to do.

THE ANGER OF JESUS

I suspect that all this speculation will do little for someone in pain or present at the pain of others. So I turn to the example of Jesus to respond yet again to the question 'Where is God when it hurts?' The Christ of the gospels gives us the key. In Jesus God enters into our world. By becoming a human being he experiences our pain from the inside. We know this only too well, of course. The technical term, incarnation, has all but lost the capacity to surprise us or shock us. 'Whatever else would God do?' we think. 'Of course he became a human being.' Two thousand years of Christianity and countless carol services have dulled the scandal: 'The word was made flesh and dwelt among us.' King's College Chapel, candlelight and 'In the bleak mid-winter'. All rather beautiful really.

This was pretty much my view until I had to go into hospital for an operation. It was a minor piece of surgery but, given the nature of hospitals, I found myself lying wide awake one night listening to the noises of the ward. In the bed opposite an old man groaned more or less all the time. You know how in hospitals bodily functions take on an unreasonable importance. Everyone, patients and staff, seems obsessed with regularity, not to mention performance targets. That night, at three in the morning, I realized what it was that God took on in Jesus – 'flesh' is skin, sinew and muscle; it is also bone, sweat, urine and faeces. In Gethsemane Jesus knows pain. He is in anguish and his sweat is like drops of blood. All his life he knows what it is to be tired, hungry and to thirst; and when he bleeds he bleeds real blood.

There is more. Two incidents in the gospels shed an extraordinary light on how Jesus saw the pain of others.

The first is the account of his meeting with a leper in Mark's gospel (Mark 1:40–5). The leper comes in haste, falling to his knees in front of Jesus and begging him to listen to him. 'If you want to', he says, 'you can make me clean.' Most versions of the story follow the leper's plea with the phrase 'Jesus was filled with compassion'. But an alternative reading in the manuscripts gives the translation 'he was angry'. This is a more difficult reading and translators have to make a choice. 'Compassion' or 'anger'? Which is the correct one? Usually the sound move is to go for the more difficult reading on the grounds that that is the one most likely to have been softened. It would be unusual for a scribe to create problems by following the reverse procedure. So Jesus is *angry* in the presence of the leper. But why?

It cannot be that Jesus is angry at the leper, since he heals him. We are left with the conclusion that the anger is directed against the disease or, better, against a world where a human being can be so broken. In verse 43 Jesus 'snorts' – another unusual word. It is actually the noise made by a horse. Is it a cry of exasperation? I begin to catch a glimpse of a Jesus who is not afraid to show his emotions. He is not cold, calculating, dispassionate, or the dispenser of good advice. Here is a Jesus who gets his hands dirty, who feels pain deeply and expresses anger, urgency and energy. He is the very embodiment of the God who is *for* us. We see a Jesus who groans that any child of God should be so damaged, that society should be so uncaring and religion so powerless to help. 'Compassionate' is a powerful description of Jesus and I like the translation by Dick France: 'Jesus was churned up inside'. But I return again and again to the image of *anger*. Once I preached on this reading of the text and a man stopped at the door of the church after the service. His wife was seriously ill with cancer. 'I'll go with the God who snorts and is angry any time,' he said.

The second incident takes place before the tomb of Lazarus (John 11:33,38). Most English translations run along these lines: 'When Jesus saw her [Mary] weeping, and the Jews who had come along with her also weeping, he was deeply moved in spirit and troubled.' But it is possible to translate these words as 'angry in spirit and very agitated'. It is fascinating to see how English translations have gone for the softer rendering: 'groaned in spirit', 'sighed heavily', 'deeply moved', 'in great distress'. By contrast, German translations since Luther have preferred 'angry' or 'indignant'. Is this just a case of English politeness? We prefer a Jesus with gentler emotions, a sensitive soul, easily wounded but not likely to show much in the way of passion. It is a relief to open the commentary by Kingsley Barrett and find 'it is beyond question that (the Greek word) implies anger'[1]. Now I encounter a Jesus who before the tomb of his dead friend, even though he knows that he will shortly raise him to life, is in turmoil, shows anger, sheds tears. Why? Because none of this – death, decay, grief, loss – was meant to be.

When my father was dying I spent most of the day before he actually died holding him physically as tightly as I could. He

---

[1] C. K. Barrett, *The Gospel according to St John*, London, SPCK, 2nd edn, 1978, p. 399.

was dying of lung cancer and, somehow, being gripped around his chest seemed to ease the pain. My feelings during that day were not primarily those of sadness – they came later. As I remember the occasion I felt an overwhelming anger. He had been the kind of man who grabbed life by the throat. We used to tease him that, when any gadget needed to be assembled, if all else failed he would read the instructions. I was angry because someone so vital had been brought so low at the last. But in those circumstances, it is a comfort to know that as you sit in anger at one side of the bed, your anger is shared by Jesus who sits across on the other side.

Only the Suffering God Can Help

But there is more. How deeply will God enter into our condition? The answer seems to be 'completely'.

I once was given a training manual for politicians who have to appear on television. It was an enlightening read. One piece of advice that stuck in my mind was the importance of the 'out line'. I gathered that the out line is that one phrase that sums up everything you want to be remembered when the interview is over. It represents the essence of what you want to say and probably constitutes the reason why you agreed to be interviewed at all. At a pinch you may ignore the questions the interviewer asks as long as you include your out line. As I was studying Mark's account of the crucifixion at the time, I noticed how, as Mark tells the story, Jesus dies utterly abandoned, spurned by friends, bystanders, authorities and both thieves. Every element that softens the picture in the other gospels is lacking. In this bleak version of Good Friday, what is the out line that sums up what it is all about? It's a question: 'My God, my God, why have you forsaken me?' Jesus feels deserted even by his Father. The fracture is in some way present within the Godhead. And this cry of dereliction is met with total silence from heaven.

Camus wrote, 'The Godhead, visibly renouncing all inherited privileges, endures to the end the anguish of death, including the depths of despair. This is the explanation of the *Lama sabachthani* and Christ's gruesome doubt in agony. The agony would have been easy if it could have been supported by eternal hope. But for God to be a man, he had to despair.'[2]

'For God to be a man, he had to despair.' The letter to the Hebrews says, 'For we do not have a high priest who is unable to sympathize with our weaknesses' (Hebrews 4:15). Nor do we have a God who 'treads his way over corpses'. A colleague of mine was seriously ill and admitted to hospital. His bishop thoughtfully sent him a card, wishing him well and praying that he would know the presence of God throughout his ordeal. It was a kind gesture. But writing about his experience my friend reflects that 'at a point where one very much needs a sense of God's presence, there comes a real sense of absence as there is no room for anything or anyone in the self-absorption of pain'.[3]

Where is God when it hurts? The Christian answer has always been 'on the cross'. When the church where I presently worship was reordered in the 1980s, the architect designed an enormous cross made of black metal, as if made up of steel girders. The nails at each of the arms and at the foot have been unnaturally elongated to about twelve inches. At the intersection of crosspiece and upright a square metallic crown of thorns has been fastened. It has teeth like a mantrap. The effect is brutal and savage. This cross is suspended high up at the east end of the church against a glass screen. So Christ is flung out into the sky, spreadeagled between heaven and earth, hanging there as a sign for all who are in pain. In the course of a week dozens of visitors come into this church, many of them carrying their own hard knot of pain inside. How many notice the cross hanging high above their heads? How many sense that this image holds the secret of their healing? How many

---

2 A. Camus, *L'homme revolte*, pp. 50–51, quoted from Jürgen Moltmann, *The Crucified God*, London, SCM Press, 1974, p. 226.
3 Alan Heaton, 'An experience of pain', in *Fairacres Chronicle*, vol. xxxiii, no 1 (Spring 2000), p. 9.

feel the power of the symbol but find that its significance eludes them?

The German theologian, Dietrich Bonhoeffer, said, 'Only the suffering God can help.' In the early fifteenth century Matthias Grünewald painted a crucifixion for the hermits of St Anthony at Isenheim. It was an altarpiece and hung in the chapel of the monastery which, at the outbreak of plague, soon became a hospice for the victims of the terrible disease known as St Anthony's fire. The sufferers were taken into the chapel to die, so that this image was probably their last sight on earth. Grünewald's portrait of Christ has lost none of its horror over the centuries. The figure on the cross is modelled on the sufferings of someone afflicted with St Anthony's fire. The body is blackened with the marks of the scourging, the skin a mass of greenish, suppurating sores. Christ's flesh is covered with spiteful scratches, needle pricks of pain, as if someone had worked systematically over the body scratching it with thorns or cutting it with a razor blade.

Why did this sight bring comfort to those who were themselves in excruciating pain? Perhaps because they knew then that they were not called to suffer alone. They knew that once God too had cried out in agony. Sheila Cassidy tells of a Bible found in a detention centre in Chile. An unknown Christian, the victim of the secret police, had written in it: 'I could only close my eyes and hold his hand and grit my teeth and know with that cold, dark, naked knowing that He was there.'

And there is more. Where is God when it hurts? I suggest that he is feeling the pain with us. This phrase might mean, if one can speak in this way, no more than that the Father 'remembers' the crucifixion or that Christ 'remembers' what the pain was like. I want to go further than this, however. The person that is me is enshrined in my body. If the physical me is in pain then the person that is me feels it. The pain is not a concept or an idea; it is felt for real. The pain of the body is not to be detached from the person who feels it. If God is related to his world as my person is related to my body, if he is, in some important sense, *inside* his creation, then perhaps we can glimpse the possibility that he feels its pain. This is more than saying, 'God understands' or 'God has suffered'; it is to assert that God feels our pain *when we feel* it. He suffers with the child dying of Down's syndrome, with the old woman whimpering in a hospital bed or the victim of brutality in prison. Where is God when it hurts? If the creation groans in pain, then God will not do less. The wounds of Christ are fresh. They are not scars. They still bleed.

Like Wheat That Springeth Green

There is one thing more to say. We are not left only with a suffering God, impotently wringing his hands. I was taken aback at the vehemence with which one man said to me, 'I need a suffering God like a hole in the head!' In a future chapter I want to explore the *hope* we have in Christ – a hope of a new creation, when sorrow and sighing and tears will be done away, when the lame shall leap like a hart and the tongue of the dumb sing. For the moment let me anticipate that chapter and declare that the suffering God is not the end of the matter. Paul exults that the afflictions of the present time are not worthy to be compared with the glory that shall be revealed.

To us Christ says, 'Trust this hope. Rest your weight on it.' I read recently of an interview with a young man who was severely disabled. The questioner asked, 'Don't you feel bitter?' Apparently he grinned. 'God has all eternity to make it up to me,' he said. Is this pie in the sky when you die? I hope not. Certainly, *without* this hope we have been abandoned in a cold, unfeeling universe, working out its course of decay, disease, cruelty and death, the product of randomness or sadism, without purpose or meaning, except the meaning of the madhouse or the torture chamber. That last sentence may read like a sentence of death, but the truth is that we have *not* been abandoned. The final comment on our world and ourselves belongs to the Easter hymn 'Love is come again like wheat that springeth green'.

REFLECTION

When people ask, 'Why does God allow suffering?' what sort of answer are they looking for?

When have you sensed that your mistakes have been woven into God's pattern?

Does the picture of 'the angry Christ' help? How might it change our response to our own suffering and that of others?

'At a point where one very much needs a sense of God's presence, there comes a real sense of absence as there is no room for anything or anyone in the self-absorption of pain.' What can you do when this happens – for yourself or for others?

MEDITATION

For this you need to close your eyes and take a journey of imagination.

You're in a kind of workshop. It's for making stained-glass windows. All around you are designs for windows and areas where glass is being measured and cut.

On the table in front of you lie pieces of broken glass. All kinds of colours. Sharp edged.

Christ is standing at your side. It is his workshop.

He says, 'These are your hurts, your griefs; these are the pains you feel, each one a splinter of broken glass.'

Even here in the presence of Christ you can hardly bear to touch them. They have cut you too deeply in the past.

But you recognize each piece. Gently, Christ asks you to name them.

Tell him where it hurts. And why. And who.

He is listening. Now he takes each piece and begins to arrange them on the table. Fitting them together. Making a pattern for a new window – taking your hurt and shaping it into something beautiful.

A Prayer Exercise

When life hurts and prayer is really difficult, a prayer partner can be a great help. Take time to pray with a trusted friend using the words below. Ask your prayer partner to say the words of reassurance after you have prayed about what is causing you pain.

A prayer for you to say:

Lord, where are you when it hurts?
Where are you when ...? [Say why you are hurting.]

For your prayer partner to say:

The Lord says:
'I am beside you.
I am on the cross.
I am feeling the pain with you.
Nothing can separate you from my love.'

O Christ, by means of tears and sweat and blood you
    made a poem out of bitterness. You know that when
    we hurt we want to hide.
We give to you our grief, our fear, our anger, and our loss.
Keep us from dry eyes and cold hearts,
the numbness that cannot grieve;
and the deadness that will not feel.
And take our pain and make it something beautiful.

CHAPTER 7

THE COSMIC SAVIOUR

D read comes in many shapes and sizes. It's the nameless horror of which panic attacks are made. It's the dark shadow that comes silently into the bedroom at three in the morning and stands watching you lie there rigid with terror. It's the anxiety that grips your entrails when you hear of the death of someone your age and leads you to promise to be nicer to your family so that the avenging angel will pass you by. It's the fear you felt as a child when you thought you might escape the nightmare, if only you could avoid stepping on the cracks in the pavement. Sometimes it's the fear that if you move only a little from where you stand, a hole will open up in the universe and you will fall into it and go on falling endlessly. Dread comes in all shapes and sizes.

Dread is nastier than fear; it has to do with our existence. Dread is ultimate threat, the worst of fears, the sinking feeling that the future might not be orange so much as impenetrable black. A jolly little book called *The Paranoid's Pocket Guide* shows us dread *domesticated*.[1] It contains all the little things you might be worrying about and is actually very funny. But it also reminds us of the taste of dread, so that we laugh, but nervously. What do you make of fears like 'The drycleaner smells my clothes'? Or, 'Everything my mother has ever told me about my appearance is true'? One ghoulish example informs the reader, 'When you dry off with a towel, dead skin cells cling to its surface, providing protein to feed micro-organisms such as *Staphylococcus aureus*, which can cause infection and pustules. Even the clean towel you used last night will be crawling with organisms by the time you use it

---

1 Cameron Tuttle, *The Paranoid's Pocket Guide*, San Francisco, Chronicle Books, 1997.

this morning.' This is on a level with the television documentary on building and decorating that ended with a shot of a couple sitting by their living room fire while the soundtrack carried the amplified noise of all the creepy crawlies which at that very moment were eating the building.

This is the stuff of which the *Alien* films are made. They tap into a primal horror. Edvard Munch's picture *The Scream* is a profoundly disturbing vision of what the world looks like when Dread takes over. A man stands at what looks like a long jetty. In the distance stand other figures but they are detached and uninvolved. The man's face is distorted in a ghastly rictus of pain. The scream issuing from his mouth fills the canvas, writhing and twisting – a terrible picture of what it feels like to be lost, of a universe tearing apart, of a human being about to fall into the abyss.

SAVING FOR A RAINY DAY

Christianity is a salvation religion; the very name 'Jesus' means saviour. But what does the phrase 'Jesus saves' *mean* in our world? We know the graffiti 'Jesus saves – with the Woolwich, of course' and 'Jesus saves – but Michael Owen scores on the rebound', but what can 'Jesus saves' mean to people who are not sure what he saves them from or why they need saving? Conventionally, what gets saved is the soul, an insubstantial ghost, rather like cigarette smoke, which gets laundered and sent to play a harp on a planet called heaven, a little to the left of Alpha Centauri. It's too much like an advert for washing powder. Not that our age knows nothing of dread, angst and desperation. Film-makers regularly produce visions of contemporary hells, but the prospect of a whiter than white soul doesn't seem big enough to meet the problem. The great requiems contain the prayer 'Libera me, Domine, de morte aeterna' – 'Deliver me, O Lord, from eternal death.' Now that's real dread.

Tomorrow Is Not a Place to Be

'If it ain't broke, don't fix it' goes the saying. Before we call the fire engine, we ought to make sure there is a fire. So what meaning can we give to 'eternal death', how can God deliver from death, and what does it mean to be a lost soul? How are we to describe the predicament into which humanity has fallen? Are Christians just naturally gloomy? In Douglas Coupland's novel *Girlfriend in a Coma*, Karen, the girl of the title, just before going into a coma, foresees something that terrifies her. Her boyfriend muses:

> She saw a picture, however fragmentary, that told her that tomorrow was not a place she wanted to visit – that the future is not a place in which to be. This is what haunted me – the thought that maybe she was right.[2]

Earlier another schoolfriend called Jared, who is actually dead as he speaks, addresses his friends:

> Back to right now – here, where I am, here at world's end. Yes, the world is over. It's still *here* but it's ... *over*. I'm at the End of the World. Dust in the wind. The end of the world as we know it. Just another brick in the wall. It sounds glamorous but it's not. It's dreary and quiet and the air always smells like there's a tire fire half a mile up wind.[3]

Tomorrow is not a place she wants to visit. What's gone wrong? Where's the problem? Of the dozens of ways of describing the human condition I pick out three.

---

2 Douglas Coupland, *Girlfriend in a Coma*, London, Flamingo, 1998, p. 60.
3 Coupland, *Girlfriend in a Coma*, p. 4.

The Pointlessness of it All

It seems crystal clear that the universe will end badly. The evidence of decay and decomposition are all around us. We see a universe that is either running down like a battery at the end of its life, or gathering itself for an almighty traffic pile up. Everyone grows old, despite liposuction, cryogenics and visits to the health club. Alzheimer's and other forms of dementia are so common that we are no longer surprised to witness the slow erosion of every faculty that makes an individual recognizable. And death comes even to golden lads and lasses. The scientist Peter Atkins ends *The Second Law* with the words 'We are the children of chaos and the deep structure of change is decay. At root, there is only corruption, and the unstemmable tide of chaos. Gone is purpose; all that is left is direction. This is the bleakness we have to accept as we peer deeply and dispassionately into the heart of the Universe.'[4]

The effect of unstoppable decay on humanity is that it becomes implausible to believe in any overarching purpose. There is direction but it looks as if it is towards the precipice. Ten thousand lemmings can't be wrong. We don't know what the world is coming to? 'Only we die in earnest; that's no jest.'

Everywhere we Are in Chains

The second aspect of the human condition is a sense of being enslaved. Some years ago, Thomas Luckmann in his study of 'secular religion' sketched a picture of the autonomous self.[5] The idea of a soul, a centre to my life, is retranslated as *the real me*, an inner personality waiting to be let loose. Somewhere inside there is a self that is screaming to get out. My duty is to

---

4 P. W. Atkins, *The Second Law: Energy, Chaos, and Form*, New York, W. H. Freeman, 1994, p. 200.
5 Thomas Luckmann, *The Invisible Religion*, London, Collier-Macmillan, 1967.

nourish this real me and ensure that it develops and is released to flourish in the world. Various gurus and experts may help me in this enterprise, ranging from the weight loss adviser to the new lover that I take in preference to last year's partner.

'Finding yourself' takes on the status of the quest for the holy grail and is the central theme of many films and novels. In the works of Joanna Trollope, for example, a main character, frequently female, finds herself imprisoned and stifled by her situation – the demands of family, an unsatisfying marriage, a stultifying lifestyle – and longs to discover her true self. As the plot unfolds her real identity is revealed and latent possibilities are realized. One way or another, she finds freedom, perhaps through a radical break in her lifestyle or by awakening her slumbering sexuality, preferably with a lover in an exotic location. It is a bit cheap to dismiss these themes as 'Aga Sagas'. They explore the contemporary quest for the golden fleece.

It is possible that the same need to release the inner self is what is going on in all those deeds of daring and endurance that men and women undertake. Sailing round the world, finishing the London marathon or the Great North Run, climbing Annapurna, completing the Three Peaks, these constitute ordeals and tasks that demand everything of us as a person. They call out everything we possess by way of resources. They demand great sacrifice. Putting yourself in danger or in situations that require you to push yourself to the limits, asks hard questions of us: 'Can I do it? Can I survive? Do I have the resources within myself? Who am I underneath?' These are variants of 'Will the real me come out, please.' The motivation for climbing Everest is supposed to be 'because it's there', but perhaps it hasn't got very much to do with mountains.

Unfortunately, as we pursue the quest we often come to realize that we are in bondage – to our genes, our parents and the way they brought us up, and to our past experiences. We are not free to do whatever we set our hearts on. We are also restricted by our bank balance and manipulated by commercial interests that feed us mind-altering drugs in the form of advertising hard sells. We think we are free but are being programmed. It's common to speak of pressures at work – the rat race, the treadmill, and now 'the churn'. According to Celia Brayfield: 'Churn is a nice executive buzz-word for sheer bloody chaos and is caused by mergers, acquisitions, restructuring, relocating, downsizing, upgrading, contracting out, buying in, starting up, selling on and generally running as fast as a business can to hold its own in a competitive market.'[6] Churn is good for business. Churn is bad for people. Lunch is for wimps.

There is no need for dramatic examples of drugs and alcohol to see that there are powers and structures that seem to stifle genuine human flowering. This is even more obvious outside Europe. The Two-Thirds World is denied a genuinely human existence by poverty and oppression. The odd crash in the world money markets suggests that no one has it all sussed and that chaos may be nearer than we think. In the first century there was widespread belief that the world was ruled by unseen powers and principalities. Perhaps the belief is due for a comeback. The film *The Matrix* depicts a world where humans believe they have freedom but are in fact living in virtual reality, controlled within their dream existence by a computer-driven intelligence known as the Matrix. In a moment of terrible choice the hero opts to see into the heart of things. It is a nightmare vision of human bodies, imprisoned by a cyberspace brain without pity. Each body is simply a battery supplying heat and electrical energy to machines that control the world. Human beings are controlled and farmed objects. This is the reality of the Matrix. The tragedy is that the human beings think they are free.

PLAYING GOD

The third aspect of the human plight is a sense of alienation from other human beings. Glaring examples are easy to find –

6 Celia Brayfield, 'Worked to death', *Times* 2, 26 June 2000, p. 3.

in the gender war and the exploitation of women by men, in the growth of tribalism of different kinds, in racism and aggressive nationalism. But we don't have to go looking for it. There's plenty of nastiness behind the living-room curtains. We live in a 'put-down' society. Tabloid exposés show that we have a taste for scandal. Abuse, road rage, comedy that majors in insult and scorn rather than wit, neighbours from hell, builders from hell, holidays from hell – evidence of a cordial dislike of our fellows is easy to find. Sartre said, 'Hell is other people.' Even the television game show *The Weakest Link* is based on the entertainment value of expelling the weakest member of the group.

Alienation shows itself in a more sinister fashion when nastiness is redrawn as evil. Evil is not crime, nor breaching a social taboo, nor a lapse that leads to loss of self-esteem. Evil is a moral issue. Evil implies standards outside myself. It implies that good and bad, right and wrong are objective realities and not just personal preferences. Evil presupposes accountability. It belongs in a world of justice, remorse and regret, of guilt and not merely guilty feelings.

From time to time an act occurs that confronts us with the reality of evil, where the relativizing framework cracks. The systematic torture and murder of eight-year-old Anna Climbie opened up an abyss. In these circumstances we do not say, 'Well, it's not for me but that's the way they want to express themselves, so I suppose I shouldn't interfere or condemn.' Even atheists can be heard to say that they wish there were some place of ultimate damnation where such evils could be adequately condemned and punished.

Christians say that the root of alienation lies in the human desire to play God. If we think we are the centre of the universe and that everything revolves around us, then it's not long before we write our own script, play the starring lead and insist on being director as well. But this is not what we were designed to be. A real human life entails living as God's vice-regents on earth. Created just a little lower than the angels, we were made to walk freely in a garden, able to enjoy the fruit of every tree (except one). God longs to give us life in abundance. Personal fulfilment can be achieved in friendship with him. But to live life without acknowledging that it is held in trust from God, that it is meant to be lived in relationship with him and in obedience to him spells disaster. It is not only bad news for those we exploit; it also goes against the grain of our own being so that we are spiky and prickly with ourselves. There is no unhappier creature than the small child who is allowed to do exactly what it likes. It grows up in a lunatic world where adults leap about to satisfy its every whim. But it desperately needs limits and security. The power of its own omnipotence is terrifying and threatens to overwhelm it. Louis MacNeice's 'Prayer before birth' pleads, 'Let not the man who is beast or who thinks he is God come near me.' Playing God is the essence of sin.

Making the Best of a Bad Job

I know this makes for a gloomy picture but is it a realistic one? Is human life in a universe that is running down ultimately pointless? Are all our efforts to liberate our real selves no more than threshing about at the bottom of a deep hole? Do we always misuse our freedom and demand to be king of the cosmic castle? And if this is the size of the problem, what can God do about it?

Imagine a mother who is worn out by the fact that her two sons fight all the time. What options does she have? She can deny that anything is wrong, arguing that, after all, boys will be boys. But the shouting and screaming suggest that her sons are unhappy at heart. Perhaps she ought just to put up with it, grimly and sadly, but wincing at each crash. More theatrically, she can announce that she wants no more to do with them and abandon them to their punch-ups. She locks the door of the living room and doesn't re-enter until one or the other has overcome, bloodied but victorious, leaving an inert form on the carpet and a quantity of broken china ducks. Or she can force them into co-operation, angrily standing over them, threatening punishments if they don't speak nicely to one another. This will achieve the appearance of peace, at least while she is within earshot. There are other possibilities, of course, involving the creative use of superglue, burying them in the garden and selling them to a passing tradesman, but I shall leave these unexplored.

As an alternative to all these strategies, let us suppose that she decides to work *with* them. Now she enters the room, at one point helping them to see why they're jealous of each other, at another modelling co-operative behaviour, at another encouraging them to see each other's point of view. No doubt she is treated to complaints, accusations of favouritism and hostility.

Only one of these reactions really qualifies as *redeeming* the situation. The other responses work from outside the situation. The decision to work with the boys entails the mother coming physically into the room, putting herself out, giving time and effort to understanding the boys' way of seeing things, paying the price of being misunderstood and even being vilified. There are other kinds of cost involved – a relaxing half-hour with *Cosmopolitan* goes by the board, so does having Jenny round for coffee or redrafting a chapter of the novel she's working on. Weighing up the alternatives she may feel that 'Why don't you two go and play with the traffic?' has a certain charm. How long she is prepared to go on working with the boys is a mark of her commitment to them.

The word 'redemption' presupposes that the thing to be redeemed is worth redeeming. A broken 10p Biro is thrown in the bin. Only the conservation freak mends it with Sellotape. Redemption also assumes that the object is not so far gone that it cannot be mended – it is a sign of hope when the surgeon says, 'I think we can save the leg.' Again, the word implies that covering up the defect is not acceptable – 'papering over the cracks' suggests a shoddy, short-term device for avoiding detection. Redemption implies that things are bad (or we would not need to talk of redeeming at all), but not so far gone that all is lost.

In the analogy of the mother and the children we saw that the mother could opt to act outside the problem, or to immerse herself within it. God has taken the second course. He loves this world and believes it is worth saving and so he takes decisive action. As St Paul puts it, 'God was reconciling the world to himself in Christ' (2 Corinthians 5:19). In the person of Jesus of Nazareth God enters our problem and begins to make his superlative best of a bad job.

What God Means by a Human Life

If we hold in mind the threefold problem that confronts humanity we can see how the Jesus of the gospels is a sign of how it might be solved. He is what God means by a human being. In his healings he demonstrates that this decaying world can be broken open by the powers of the age to come. Lepers are healed, the blind see, the lame walk. These are the signs of the future. This is how it can be. His attack on the demonic demonstrates God's commitment to overthrowing all that would enslave humanity. His freedom from the red tape of the religious establishment models a way of living that obeys God rather than rules. Nor is he fearful of political might – Herod is called 'that fox' and Pilate told he could have no power unless it were given him from above. Jesus is not alienated from his fellows – all are free to come into the kingdom feasts. He crosses boundaries, receives Samaritans, Romans, women, children, tax collectors and teaches a radical new way of loving enemies. He washes his disciples' feet as a sign of a life committed to serving one's fellows. When he is faced with those who have done evil he forgives. A woman taken in adultery is sent on her way with the words 'Neither do I condemn you. Go and sin no more.' As he is nailed to the cross he prays that his Father will forgive his executioners, 'because they do not know what they are doing'. And he shows no sinful desire to rule the roost in contradiction of his Father's will.

THE POWER AND THE WEAKNESS OF GOD

However, Jesus is more than a model of what God wants humanity to be like. He actually makes salvation happen. The theological phrase 'the finished work of Christ' (hardly words to quicken the pulse) means that *he does the job*. Each part of the problem outlined earlier is dealt with through Good Friday and Easter Day.

Jesus undergoes the sharpness of death, that ultimate statement of the foolishness and meaninglessness of life. But as the hymn says, 'from the ground there blossoms red, life that shall endless be'. Life cannot now be pointless since Jesus has died and risen to a new life. Death cannot hold him. 'Thou wouldst not suffer thy Holy One to see corruption' is a statement that matter matters. In the resurrection, God promises to reclaim decaying flesh and make it something new. The body of Jesus is recognizably the body he inhabited during his ministry, but now is a resurrected body. It is not a resuscitated corpse but the promise that matter can be transformed and given by God qualities it did not possess before the coming of Christ. The exhilarating truth is that God will reconcile everything to himself in Christ – not only humanity but also the animal kingdom (from aardvarks to zebras) and matter itself (from quarks and gluons to the distant galaxies).

The powers that enslave us are also defeated on the cross, even though Jesus may seem as if he is crushed by the powers of evil and by the people and structures that serve them. He accepts all that happens to him. He bears its brunt. 'Brunt' is a strange word that means the central impact of an attack. All that evil, hatred, malice, abuse, pride and spite can throw at Jesus, he accepts. Though we call it his passion, it is his action. He absorbs the evil, and in him God absorbs it. But evil cannot have the last word. The one nailed to the cross, the very image of weakness, cannot be held in the tomb. Ezra Pound refers to Christ as 'a jack in the box'. The resurrection is God's great joke, it's the divine mockery of the powers, a laugh everlastingly let loose. The stone is rolled away and he roams freely in the world. Go in your imagination to that stone box in which the powers of this age shut God up, slamming down the lid, and listen to the words 'He is not here!' You can't keep a good God down.

What will Christ do about our alienation from each other and from God? Jesus is free to live for others. He absorbs the spitefulness of his tormentors without bitterness. His words to Judas are reproachful not abusive. He looks on Peter and still loves him. He bends his back to the whip but does not curse. From the cross itself he forgives enemies, promises life to a penitent thief and cares about his mother even in his pain. He is the man for others. Since God was in Christ then we can see God expressing his nature, which is to give himself to others even if they return hatred for love. God works this out in the arena of his world, through flesh, the medium that needs to be redeemed and through which God has chosen to work.

The idea of absorbing hurt is a model for God's encounter with evil. What will he do when humanity vents its hatred and rebellion on him? We expect a thunderbolt as the Almighty annihilates those who dare to resist his power. To crucify God is the ultimate blasphemy. Yet God allows it to happen. Is there a point beyond which God will not go? Some escape button where he cries, 'Enough is enough!'? Apparently not. He refuses to come down from the cross and call a halt to the blasphemy. But once more, God cannot be broken by sin. If he chooses to hold the contact and allow the lethal charge to flow into his own person then there is nothing humanity can do to prevent this act of grace.

There is a mystery here that resists explanation, though ordinary human relationships can shed some light on it. Imagine a husband who has betrayed his wife. His adultery has involved him in deceit and betrayal over a long period of time. His marriage has been marred by lies, broken promises and deliberate spite. Eventually, the affair is discovered. At first he denies everything and flies into a rage. When he finally admits what he has done, he speaks resentfully and with bitterness.

We may think the marriage is at an end, and from his side perhaps it is. Even if he later has a change of heart there is nothing he can do to blot out the injury he has done to his wife. He may express regret, buy expensive presents, or even take her to Paris for a holiday. But the one thing he cannot do is make himself innocent – the offence cannot be undone. His betrayal can only be dealt with *if the wife absorbs its hurt into herself*. She has to take the brute fact of his unfaithfulness into herself. He has forfeited any right to be called a faithful husband. She is the only one who can restore the situation, and she does this by continuing to love him and to give him the status he does not deserve.

Setting the death of Jesus alongside a story about marriage reminds us that what God did was not a businesslike transaction. The cross ought to touch our hearts and stir our emotions. Isaac Watts wrote his great hymn 'When I survey the wondrous cross' in order that we should *see* what Christ endured and achieved for us. In the second verse he exclaims, 'See! From his head, his hands, his feet, / sorrow and love flow mingled down!' Make sure you see it and not just talk about it. A verse later he looks again at the cross and writes the haunting lines 'his dying crimson like a robe / spreads o'er his body on the tree'. Here is love, not that we loved God, but that he loved us. 'Were the whole realm of nature mine, / that were an offering far too small.'

A Hymn to the Cosmic Christ

The story of Easter is retold as poetry by St Paul writing to the church at Colossae. In the middle of the letter he suddenly launches into a hymn to Christ who redeems the whole of creation, nature and humanity, through his death and resurrection. Like Watts, Paul hopes to move the Colossians to worship and thankfulness.

He is the image of the invisible God, the firstborn over all creation. For by him all things were created: things in heaven and on earth, visible and invisible, whether thrones or powers or rulers or authorities; all things were created by him and for him. He is before all things, and in him all things hold together. And he is the head of the body, the church; he is the beginning and the firstborn from among the dead, so that in everything he might have the supremacy. For God was pleased to have all his fulness dwell in him, and through him to reconcile to himself all things, whether things on earth or things in heaven, by making peace through his blood, shed on the cross. (Colossians 1:15–20)

The hymn is all about Christ, who is the image, or literally 'the icon', of the invisible God. Jesus is God in visible form. He is the God you can see and handle, a God handing himself over to be prodded and pushed about. Jesus is God in human flesh, expressed in a human life, in a particular place at a particular time. In Jesus we hear the divine music, a tune that we have always known but never quite been able to place, now heard in all its beauty and richness. In a daring phrase Paul says that all the fullness of God was poured into Jesus. So God inserts himself into the creation that he has made, like a life-giving serum injected into the bloodstream of a dying man. Only by coming into the world and working from the inside can he mend what is broken.

Christ is set before us as the power through which God made the universe. Everything was made through him and everything now holds together because he keeps it in existence. Christ is the reason that grass is green and that gloss paint glosses. But if we take the words seriously, it is Christ's power that sustains this now broken, flawed and decaying world and his power that holds in place the superhuman forces – described as thrones, powers, rulers, authorities – that keep humanity in slavery. Within the mystery of the love of God, Christ sustains these elements; he does not pull the plug on the whole sorry mess and let creation, powers and humanity disappear into a black hole. As we eavesdrop on this passage we sense that, perhaps, what he created he may yet be able to redeem.

The action of redemption takes place in the body of Jesus, through his cross and resurrection. There is a logic in this. If it is death and decay that make this world meaningless, if enmity between human beings shows itself in wounding words and blows, if people are trapped within their bodies, if rebellion against God is expressed in what we think in our brains and say with our lips and do with our hands, then the place where the battle must be fought is in what Paul calls, 'the body of his flesh'.

The key words in the hymn point to the way God rescues lost humanity. The fullness of the living God comes into a world dominated by death and decay. God in Christ constitutes a new element, like 'good infection' in a body. Christ is the first man to go through death, the 'first-fruits' from the dead, a sign that a vast harvest can follow. He is the 'beginning' of a new humanity, because a new kind of human being has lived a human life from start to finish without departing from the will of God. He has absorbed all the hatred of sinful human beings and so made peace 'through the blood of the cross'. He is the 'head' of a new community, a new race of human beings who will be like his body on earth, living in harmony and love. These are all pictures, of course, for the hymn works by touching our imaginations and its language is in overdrive.

GOLDEN WITH FRUIT OF A MAN'S BODY

But Paul is not content with painting a picture of the glory of the cosmic Christ. The story of how the universe came home is awe-inspiring but can it include me as well as the farthest stars and the human race? Suddenly and dramatically the good news becomes personal with the words 'Once *you*' (Colossians

1:21). 'He made you alive,' says Paul. 'You were alienated from God. Your mindset showed that you were God's enemies. You lived lives of darkness. And Christ reconciled you to God.' Of course it is a mystery but perhaps we can catch a glimpse of the yearning in God's heart for all that he has made, of the fire of love incarnated in Jesus and the paradox by which suffering has power to redeem even the hopeless situation and the lost soul. There are some lines in a poem of R. S. Thomas that I always find incredibly moving:

> Was he baulked by silence? He kneeled long,
> And saw love in a dark crown
> Of thorns blazing, and a winter tree
> Golden with fruit of a man's body.[7]

The conviction that suffering Love has enormous power surfaces in the strangest places. Reading the Harry Potter books I came across an episode where Dumbledore, the headmaster of Hogwarts Academy, a school for young wizards, explains to Harry the meaning of the mark Harry carries on his forehead. Earlier in the story the reader has learned that Harry's mother died in an attempt to shield her son from the evil Voldemort. Dumbledore explains that her love, costing not less than everything, has given Harry a kind of invisible protection. Whatever the powers of those who have sold themselves to evil, they are incapable of doing him any ultimate harm.[8]

In the summer of 2000 the National Gallery mounted an exhibition of Christian art under the title 'Seeing Salvation'. It was vastly successful and large crowds went to look at pictures produced in the main by Christian artists who wanted to express the mystery of the love of God seen in the cross. Many

---

7 R. S. Thomas, 'In a country church', in *Collected Poems 1945–1990*, London, J. M. Dent, 1995, p. 67.
8 J. K. Rowling, *Harry Potter and the Philosopher's Stone*, London, Bloomsbury, 1997, p. 216.

who attended had never seriously investigated the Christian story, so that the taped commentary had to translate even words like 'incarnation' and 'resurrection'. The success of the exhibition suggested that the story of salvation could still fire the imagination even of our secularized culture. One would like to think it was because the image of the suffering God retained its power to speak to human beings haunted by dread. The way the human plight is defined and described has changed over the centuries but perhaps creatures in free fall still hope for someone to catch them.

ON BEING AN EASTER PEOPLE

Where does that leave us? It is easy even after contemplating the love of Christ in the cross to think that the whole business is about getting answers to problems. God gives us presents: hope beyond death and decay, power to be truly free, forgiveness of sins and a new humanity. But what God really gives us is himself. All the benefits of Christ's coming, the riches of his grace and the blessings of salvation are code words for saying that God gives us himself. God has nothing else and nothing better to give us. Of course, when we receive his gift of himself, we receive all the other blessings as well, just as human friendship brings with it long walks, lunches in pubs, good conversation, a listening ear, and birthday presents. 'He brought you to life,' says Paul. God urges us to look at Jesus, 'God as one of us', doing things we could not do for ourselves. He also calls us to receive and experience him in the form of the Spirit, 'God's presence within us'. The word for 'spirit' in Greek also means 'breath'. Life comes when God breathes himself into us.

What difference does it make to live with God's breath within you? St Paul called Christ the head of the church. If he brought redemption to the world in his physical body, the body of his flesh, we shouldn't be surprised to learn that the effects of that redemption have to be worked out in flesh as well. That is why the church is called his body. A redemption that only

works in the celestial sphere, that is good only for airy creatures like angels and cherubs, will cut no ice with those who
have to struggle on in skin and bone. The church is called to
show the reality of what Christ has done, to flesh it out as he
did, to make theory and doctrine palpable, something people
can see and touch.

This sounds a tall order and the church has hardly been
spectacularly successful in its task. But you learn to ride a
bicycle by getting on every time you fall off, and Christians, of
all people, ought not to give up because of past failures. What
might embodying the good news look like? Out of literally
hundreds of examples I mention just three.

Keep the Faith

First Paul said we must take our stand on the truth that God in
Christ has reconciled the world to himself. 'Continue in the
faith' and 'do not shift from the hope of the gospel'. We are to
make this our line in the sand, the sticking place from which
we will not budge, where we say, 'This is the rock on which I
base my life.' This commitment will show itself in dozens of
ways, some of them apparently quite trivial, but all pointing to
our ultimate foundation. Saying grace at meals affirms that
God is the author of every good gift; always having wine at
Sunday lunch marks this day as special because it is the day of
the resurrection; turning up at church on a foggy November
evening, even for a boring service, affirms that this is where I
hear the words of eternal life. And, while no one wants a fixed
grin, we might as well look cheerful while we're doing all this.
The resurrection is God's joke. Let's look as if we understand
the punchline.

RESPECT THE EARTH

Then, secondly, if God has redeemed creation, Christians should be concerned about the environment. I'm impressed by those people who say by their actions, 'The world of nature was created through Christ, depends on him for its existence and will be totally transformed by him. So it's important to treat it with respect.' I am, I confess, not terribly good at this but am trying to visit the bottle bank more regularly. And, though personally they do nothing for me, I can see how gardening and birdwatching can be Christ-honouring pursuits. The sight of a kingfisher can draw the heart to worship, as Gerard Manley Hopkins knew. Maybe a bar-tailed godwit can do the same. Working the allotment can be about reclaiming the soil for God. In among the fine tilth, the mulch, the bean haulm and green wellies, we become God's partner in turning a wilderness into the garden of Eden. How we treat animals says a lot about how we see heaven. Will the world be redeemed? Is it worth redeeming? Isaiah says that the lion will lie down with the lamb one day. The cynic says, 'Yeah, but the lamb won't get much sleep.' I prefer the whimsical picture of the lion choosing the vegetarian option on the menu. So, if I am to point to the life of the world that shall be, watch how I treat my pets. We are their foretaste of heaven. I remember watching a Franciscan brother carefully extricate a mouse from the teeth of Clare, the Friary cat. He put the cat out of the back door and the mouse out of the front, then turned to me. 'It's hell being a Franciscan,' he said. But the look of pure adoration in the eyes of a dog or the noise of a rusty engine coming from a really ecstatic cat witness that here is a little bit of nature at one with humanity and not being exploited by it. So we hint at a new creation. These examples are deliberately undramatic. I am trying to suggest that faith in Christ is an all-embracing, totally overriding life-stance and because it is comprehensive we can point to it even in the minutiae of life. Witness doesn't relate only to those bits we call religious; we can give testimony to our faith in the most mundane ways.

Pursue All that Makes for Peace

There is one area of life, however, that is far from trivial. Given that God in Christ was and is primarily in the business of reconciling, perhaps the church should pay especial attention to being peacemakers. Making peace is God's work. That's why Jesus said, 'The peacemakers shall be called the children of God.' Peacemaking was Christ's agenda. He deliberately chose Matthew, a tax collector, a traitor and a collaborator, as one of his disciples. And then he put him alongside Simon, a fanatical nationalist and freedom fighter. Jesus' best-known short story is a scandalous tale of a half-caste Samaritan who dares to cross the racial divide to help a Jew. His life and death were all about breaking down barriers, dismantling the dividing walls we so carefully construct.

Those who make peace, the reconcilers, are doing God's work for him. That makes it sound very grand but usually it's very down to earth. It's about getting two friends to speak to one another again. It's about not giving up on a colleague who is silent, will not snap out of it and is obviously seething inside. Sometimes a grandparent is the perfect go between. There's no one better to say to a teenager, 'I think your dad is probably worried about you.' And to say to Dad, 'You were ten times worse when you were 16.' It's a peacemaker who says to a couple who are going through a difficult patch, 'Look, we'll have the kids for the weekend. You go off and sort it out.'

I don't think it's easy to be a reconciler. Most people think the referee is deaf, blind, of doubtful parentage and on the payroll of the other team. You have to be totally committed to both sides. And that means being fair, listening carefully, allowing for your own prejudices, helping people save face and trying to communicate someone else's point of view. And when you're locked into a conflict, whoever wants to see the other person's point of view? If you say something positive about a colleague when everyone is slagging them off, you are not voted flavour of the month.

And yet, in among the cliques and the factions, the people who aren't speaking, the office gossip, the troublemakers, stirrers and rumour mongers; those who love a crisis and delight in turning the whisper of a rumour into banner headlines; those who cannot keep confidences and those who simply tell lies, those who get from nought to lift-off in ten seconds, and those who sit silent in an Arctic fury – among all these, don't you just long for the person who seeks peace and tries to get people talking to each other? That person is the reconciler, the one who does God's work. If Christians can't be like that, God help us.

REFLECTION

In your opinion, what films or novels have most fruitfully explored the human condition and images of salvation?

How would you answer the criticism that talk of salvation is just 'pie in the sky when you die'?

This chapter argues that salvation is about deliverance from pointlessness, slavery and alienation from one another and from God. How can the lives of Christians reflect the truth of this?

MEDITATION

You might like to explore the idea of reconciliation through a guided meditation. Imagine that you're sitting round a table with two other people. You sit along one side, the others at each end.

Glance at their faces. These are two people at odds with one another. They're tense, strained, angry, resentful. Hardly able to look at one another. Staring at their fingers.

It's not a long table and you can see the hands of your companions resting on it. You know these hands very well.

Perhaps they belong to members of your family. Perhaps they're the hands of colleagues or friends or church members. Old, young; black, white; male, female. And the hands are tightly clenched, knuckles white. Unyielding, implacable.

Stretch out and put your hands on top of theirs. Feel the fingers relax. The tightly clenched fist relents almost imperceptibly. Feel the antagonism and the bitterness flow out of them and into you. Let it come.

Hold them there in the presence of Christ, and you a bridge between them.

PRAYER

O Christ, you stretched out your arms on the cross
to reconcile one to another and bring peace in place of
    strife.
Make us men and women of peace.
Give us your courage that we may answer the call to be
    reconcilers.
Give us your love that we may be swift to hear and slow
    to judge.
Give us your wisdom that we may know when to speak
    and when to be silent.
Give us your patience to persist until the task is done.

CHAPTER 8

THE ALPHA AND OMEGA

Have you ever wanted to write down your *full* address? I know this sounds strange but the last time I asked the question in public, four people showed immediately that they understood what I meant. Their slightly embarrassed smiles gave the game away. They'd obviously done exactly what I used to do as a boy. Inside the front cover of my school books I would write something like: David Day, 14 Kimblesworth Road, Tottenham, London, N17, Middlesex, Great Britain, Europe, Northern Hemisphere, Earth, the Solar System, The Milky Way, This Universe, All other Universes. It looked like a challenge to the Post Office. 'Now deliver my mail to the wrong house, if you dare!'

Most of us want to locate ourselves somewhere within a framework. When I first read James Joyce's *A Portrait of the Artist as a Young Man* I was fascinated to see that the hero Stephen Dedalus writes in the front of his geography book: Stephen Dedalus, Class of Elements, Clongowes Wood College, Sallins, County Kildare, Ireland, Europe, The World, The Universe. His classmate Fleming writes on the opposite page:

> Stephen Dedalus is my name,
> Ireland is my nation,
> Clongowes is my dwellingplace,
> And heaven my expectation.[1]

Reflecting on this Stephen asks himself, 'What was after the universe? Nothing. But was there anything round the universe

---

[1] James Joyce, *A Portrait of the Artist as a Young Man*, Harmondsworth, Penguin Books, 1969, pp. 15–16.

to show where it stopped before the nothing place began? It could not be a wall, but there could be a thin line there all round everything.' In the end he concludes, 'It made him very tired to think that way.'

WHY IS THERE ANYTHING AT ALL?

Well, it does make you tired but it seems to be a necessary exercise. Wanting to plot your position in time and space is a way of asking about the meaning of Life and the meaning of one's own life. 'Where am I?' is brother to 'Who am I?' Unfortunately, postcodes may be able to provide us with an exact address but they are less useful once you step out of your country of residence into the universe. We feel for Pascal when he said, 'The eternal silence of these infinite spaces frightens me.' The sixties song wails, 'What's it all about Alfie?' It's a fair question and one that probably doesn't go away when you consider the size of the universe in which we're trying to plot our position:

> Astronomers measure it [the universe] in 'light years' and 'light hours'. Our galaxy of stars is 100,000 light years wide. The nearest star to our own sun is 4.5 light years away. Our solar system itself is eleven light hours wide. A light year is the distance light can travel in one year, travelling at 299,728 kilometres per second (186,282 miles per second). So one light year is 9,411,109,000,000 kilometres or 5,874,600,000,000 miles (and one light hour is 1,079.028,000 kilometres or 670,620,000 miles). That's big. The universe itself is bigger.[2]

It would be odd if we didn't echo the psalmist:

---

2 Jeff Astley and David Day, *Beyond the Here and Now*, Oxford, Lion Publishing, 1996, p. 26.

When I consider your heavens,
the work of your fingers,
the moon and stars,
which you have set in place,
what is man that you are mindful of him,
the son of man that you care for him? (Psalm 8:3,4)

We appear not to be able to stop asking the big questions.

Of course, there is a rumour to the contrary. Many say confidently that questions about ultimate meaning have more or less vanished from our conversation. We ask only, 'How does it work?', 'Why has it gone wrong?', 'Did it fall off a lorry?', 'How much does it cost?' We are offered a picture of people who do not think beyond the latest quiz programme or night out, whose minds are full of this week's pub quiz or makeover, or the holiday abroad, or decorating the house, or *Vogue* or *Men's Health* or *Pigbreeders Weekly*.

But Don Cupitt's recent studies of folk theology in everyday speech, show that the habit of asking ultimate questions is alive and well. We still ask, 'What does it all add up to?', 'What's it all in aid of?', 'Where will it all end?', 'I can't make any sense of it.'[3] Everyday conversation is saturated with ultimate questions.

In his first book Cupitt examines about 150 life idioms and notes how they constitute a kind of secular theology where the word 'life' has begun to take over from 'God'. In a later volume he notes how the words 'It' and 'It All' are used to express current understandings of the human condition. Behind the commonest phrases lie implicit cosmic perspectives. Everyday speech throws up questions of meaning (Surely there's more to life than this? Is it worth it?), assumptions about fate and destiny (It just wasn't to be), faith in a future resolution of life's problems (It'll turn out all right in the end), convictions about the real purpose of human existence (Get a life; Don't miss out

---

3 See Don Cupitt, *The New Religion of Life in Everyday Speech* and *The Meaning of it All in Everyday Speech*, London, SCM Press, 1999.

on life; Something to live for; My life isn't going anywhere; I feel as if life's passed me by), and bewildered resignation (Life's like that; Life's a bitch). In Cupitt's view 'the word "God" has largely disappeared from common speech, and the old religious language, attitudes, feelings and rituals have increasingly come to be refocused around *life*.'[4]

Cupitt's research is useful because it puts a question mark against the too-ready assertion that people no longer ask ultimate questions and no longer concern themselves with looking for meaning in life. In fact, it supports the Christian assumption that we are such creatures as ruminate upon their existence. Why am I here? What's it all about? What is the right way to live? Whom can I believe? How can I be happy? Is there any point? What does it mean to do the best for my children? Is there a God? How can I face death?

I remember a biology teacher bursting into the staff room one break, exasperated by a brush he'd just had with a pupil. The class had been studying the life cycle of the frog (the way you do). He'd told them to draw a diagram in their books from frogspawn to jumping frog via tadpole, and so on, and to colour it in with their felt-tip pens. One girl was not disposed to go along with this. 'But what's it all about?' she cried. 'Look, it just goes round and round, round and round. What's it all about?' He said, 'Stop asking silly questions and get it down or you'll stay in at break.' It's an understandable reaction when faced with an adolescent philosopher, but she was right to ask the question and he was wrong to squash it.

Animals do not ask these questions. Cats do not grieve over their sins. We are the ones who agonize on Monday mornings, with our hands in the basin, and at late-night parties amid the debris of goodwill. As we stare myopically into the mirror or tipsily sing, 'Auld Lang Syne', we wonder, if only fleetingly, what it all amounts to. The author of Ecclesiastes put a different spin on our reflections. We think this way, he says,

---

4 Cupitt, *The New Religion of Life*, p. 2.

because God 'has set eternity in the hearts of men' – and women (Ecclesiastes 3:11).

It is sometimes disconcerting to find how ordinary experience can plunge us into agonizing about meaning. A personal crisis or a failure or a moment of extreme happiness or a memory can do it. Bereavement or serious illness, any kind of break-up or loss, a birth or a family wedding, a Christmas carol reminding us of more innocent times, a snatch of a song from our teenage years – all have the capacity to perforate the outer skin of our lives. Inside, where the thinking and the feeling goes on, we want to know where we stand.

In the film *Educating Rita*, Rita and her mother are sitting with friends and family in the pub. An old fashioned sing-song is going on but Rita's mother is not taking part. The camera moves in for a close-up of her face. She turns to Rita and says wistfully, 'There's got to be a better song to sing than this.' More recently *American Beauty* has dissected the American dream of Mom, apple pie and wholesome family life in the suburban dream. The film begins with the voice-over of Lester Burnham, the central character: 'I'm forty-two. In less than a year I shall be dead. Of course, I don't know that yet. And in a way, I'm dead already.'

It is possible to try to drown the inner voice. An article in the leisure section of *The Times* for 7 August 2000 prattles away:

> Make this the week that you party. Have a *fête-champêtre* on the *Île de France*, fly to Havana and salsa the night away, put flowers in your hair and throw a Bacchanalian orgy in an Attic olive grove. Why not slip on a boob tube and trip the light fantastic at your nearest night club?[5]

---

5 James Collard, 'Make this the week that you party', in *The Times*, 7 August 2000, p. 11.

Well, all right. I suppose I could. But why? Even this piece ends with a sepulchral comment: 'Because you're a long time dead, sweetie.'

In a perceptive piece about being a parent today, the actress Imogen Stubbs uncovers the unease many adults feel about their responsibilities to their children:

> Hand the remote control over to them if you must. But what will happen when tired of accruing facts, jargon, logos, trivia, soundbites and cool material trophies, weary of the quick fix, and the noise and rush of people skimming between experiences in case they're missing something more exciting, they dare to stop and reflect and ask us: 'If life is only about getting from now until death as lucratively and divertingly as possible – what is the point? Why didn't you prepare us for the questions? How do I access immortality dot-com?'[6]

COSMIC MAPS, BIG STORIES AND PACKAGE DEALS

Of course, asking ultimate questions does not necessarily mean that we are happy with the answers. For many people the world feels like an enormous hypermarket. They stand bewildered in one of the malls of the shopping centre in front of dozens of different maps. Each map has an arrow on it, confidently proclaiming, 'You are here'. But if all the maps are different, what then? It is now common to call our society postmodern. In consequence it has become much more difficult to gain a hearing even for the idea that one Cosmic Map might hold the key to the riddle of existence. The Big Stories of the universe and our place within it have been banished to a

---

6 Imogen Stubbs, 'History and culture? They're like so "not now" ', in *Times 2*, 22 August 2000, p. 9.

modernist past and are all suspect, whether they come from religious storytellers or the mythmakers of scientific progress.

Nevertheless, as far as I can tell, Big Stories continue to make claims on people's loyalties. It is not just that Christians, Muslims, Jews, Hindus, Sikhs and Buddhists have stories that deal with the meaning of all that there is, the nature of reality, the purpose of human life and the future of the universe; purveyors of popular science, followers of New Age beliefs and enthusiasts for alternative medicine also tell Big Stories even if they present only part of the total picture at a time. For example, the philosopher of science, Richard Dawkins, tells the story of the universe with passion and evangelical fervour, disposing of religion, superstition and magic along the way and preaching the good news of neo-Darwinism. The enthusiasm with which his books have been received suggests that the idea of a Grand Story of the universe has not yet been deemed unthinkable. But even a coffee-table book on *Putting Feng Shui to work in your living room* contains in little hints and nudges a total view of the way ordinary life is affected by unseen cosmic forces and powers.

Perhaps what really marks out our society is not the presence of big stories but our reluctance to accept a package deal. It is as if people say, 'You tell your Grand Narratives of the universe and we will take what appeals to us and leave the rest.' So they construct their own big picture, a DIY customized cosmos, by taking bits and pieces, bric-à-brac, flotsam and jetsam from anywhere they can find it. Like birds making their nests, they snap up unconsidered trifles from any rubbish tip that happens to be handy. The wise sayings of the ages become fashion accessories, picked out like a scarf, a belt and matching shoes, to suit their taste and image.

This means that the visit to the metaphysical sweet counter goes something like this:

'Fancy a bit of Marxism?' 'Well, only the one ... Put some Methodism in though, for Gran ... and a bit of C of E as it's nearly Christmas ... and some Zen Buddhism for Ian (looks good, I'll have a couple myself) ... and what else is there ...? 'The atheist drops look nice.' 'OK, let's try some.'[7]

There are problems here. Can you defend taking bits from different *and contradictory* big pictures just because they suit you and bring you comfort? Can you say, 'I think I shall come back as a fly or a dog or cat,' and ignore the fact that the doctrine of Samsara is embedded in a vision of reality that depicts reincarnation as a curse, not a jolly recycling of your molecules. Can you say, 'Let's get the Feng Shui expert in to design our living room,' and ignore the fact that Feng Shui assumes a total view of life as affected by unseen forces and powers? Do you really believe that putting a mirror in the hall is going to ensure that you don't wake the sleeping dragon? Or, as someone said to me once, do you think putting the toilet seat down is going to stop the force escaping? One super-market chain has begun to sell kitchen rolls with the Yin Yang symbols on them, completely detached from the belief system in which Yin Yang operates. But then, a friend tells me that when his sister was in the jeweller's looking for a necklace the assistant offered her a crucifix with the words, 'Or you can have one with a little man on it.' We know that we have fash-ioned these stories ourselves. It's rather like cheating at patience. Who are we fooling? Can such DIY pictures really help us with the big questions?

BEHIND THE SCENES AND BEYOND THE PRESENT

Meanwhile we go on needing to know what it's all about. We would like something to help us get beneath the surface, or behind the scenes, or beyond the present moment. One of the attractive aspects of Christ is that he offers us a Big Story that tells the story of the universe from creation to consummation

---

7 Astley and Day, *Beyond the Here and Now*, p. 63.

and gives us a place within its unfolding purpose. As we discover who and where we are and what we are meant to be, so life falls into place; we gain a perspective that satisfies our immortal longings and gives us direction, value and purpose. All this is no more than another example of the truth 'Without a vision the people perish'.

In the book of the Revelation, the last book of the Bible, the Christian story is set out in the form of moving pictures. The Greek word for Revelation is *Apocalypse*, which doesn't mean disaster, despite the way we use 'apocalyptic' today. The word really suggests a curtain being drawn aside to reveal what is behind it. So this book addresses our need to get behind or beneath what is happening. We long for a glimpse of what is really going on. There, in that hidden and inaccessible place, the true meaning of everything can be read off. What has been puzzling, incoherent and ambiguous up to that point suddenly displays order, sequence and pattern. Everything falls into place. We say things like 'I see how it all fits together now.'

'Getting behind' or 'beneath' is one way of putting it. We can express the same impulse for a revelatory experience as 'getting beyond'. Very often we can make no sense of what is going on until we get beyond the present moment, until we see how it all turns out in the end. The meaning is hidden in the future and the end of the story gives us a vantage point from which we can see the whole plot and therefore the meaning of any of its parts.

This is exactly what happens in our house when we have watched some particularly convoluted detective film. Hardly have the closing credits finished scrolling up the screen than we have to rerun the video in order to comprehend (for the first time, I'm afraid!) the five disconnected and baffling opening sequences. In the world of Agatha Christie Act V always reveals that the amiable, slightly dotty old man in Act I was in fact the cunningly disguised long-lost, extremely wealthy twin sister of the penniless and harassed mother of three who so caught our sympathies early on in the play. To the gasps of the astonished audience true identities are revealed and the meaning of some enigmatic and puzzling remarks are finally disclosed.

Unveiling the Mystery

In the book of Revelation we read how St John, the visionary, responds to humanity's search for meaning. We get behind the scenes and see what is really going on. We are privileged to read the last page of the story. The Christ of the book of Revelation declares, 'I am Alpha and Omega, the first and the last, the beginning and the end.' He is the brackets within which everything takes place. Nothing can fall outside these limits. Whatever happens, happens inside his sphere of power and authority. This is the inside story of the universe.

The fourth chapter of the book begins with an open door in heaven. This is just what we all long for. Just give us a glimpse behind the scenes; show us how everything will turn out in the end. Then we shall be able to live courageously and purposefully in the world on this side of the curtain.

As we read on we discover that at the centre of the picture is the vision of God, the Ruler of all, 'the one who sits upon the throne', the Eternal one, for 'He was and is and is to come'. He is presented as creator and sustainer, since 'by his will all things exist' and is a figure both of glory (in appearance like precious jewels, circled by a rainbow) and majesty (surrounded by thunder, lightning and fire). Living creatures are there, modelled on Old Testament imagery found in the prophets Ezekiel and Isaiah and suggestive of the Seraphim and Cherubim who surround and support the throne of God, give glory and honour and thanks to God. Also surrounding the throne are twenty-four elders who bow down in worship and cast their crowns before Him. Most commentators identify the creatures with the created universe and the elders with the people of God. The scene is a freeze-frame of the way the universe is ordered, with God at the centre and the creation and the church orienting themselves towards him in worship.

At the beginning of chapter 5 the picture starts to move. In a dreamlike sequence the focus shifts from the One who sits upon the throne to the scroll he holds in his hand. The scroll, written on the inside and the back, clearly a document of some length, is the story of the universe, the Master Plan that will reveal all that is about to happen and will at its end disclose the inner meaning of everything now obscure. But this Big Story is sealed with seven seals, beyond the power of anyone to break open and read. As God holds the scroll aloft we, the readers, are devastated to find that, once again, the riddle of life is beyond our understanding. We sense that there is some meaning in 'It All'; indeed we can see the solution to our agonized questionings there in the hand of God, but the secret is beyond us, indecipherable, out of reach, everlastingly and literally a closed book.

It is at this point that John begins to weep:

'I wept and wept because no-one was found who was worthy to open the scroll or look inside' (5:4). It is a literary master stroke. For his tears are the tears of all humanity. John weeps for us and for all who cry out to a faceless heaven for some small evidence of meaning in an incoherent universe. He weeps for all who sit by the hospital bed or stand by the grave. For those who read in the morning headlines about famine, torture, child abuse, earthquakes, floods and the atrocities of war and can do no more than write a cheque for a modest amount to a relief agency of their choice. He weeps for those who sit in quiet despair because their world has collapsed, who try to trace meaning in the bottom of a glass or in the tangle of the mind, but can find neither rhyme nor reason; for those who stare vacantly at the flickering screen or try to lose themselves in the relentless pursuit of pleasure. John weeps for those who dismiss life's riddle with Woody Allen's words, 'Life's a bitch and then you die.'

The Triumph of the Lamb

'Then one of the elders said to me, "Do not weep! See, the Lion of the tribe of Judah, the Root of David, has triumphed"' (5:5). Commenting on this passage, G. B. Caird makes the brilliant distinction between what John hears and what he sees.[8] He *hears* about the Lion of Judah. And then between the throne and the four living creatures he *sees* a Lamb, standing as though it had been slain. He hears about a Lion, but he sees a Lamb. So exactly, we are confronted with meekness and majesty. The Lion has conquered but the victory is won by God entering our world in humility and vulnerability and conquering through enduring death. Christ takes into himself all the hatred and anger and sinful rebellion of humanity and absorbs its impact, drawing its sting. The inside story of the universe is God in Christ reconciling the world to himself by means of the cross and resurrection. This is the big story. Christ has died, Christ is risen, Christ will come again.

The lamb has seven eyes, a symbol of the fact that to him 'all hearts are open, all desires known and from him no secrets are hidden.' He has seven horns, symbol of supreme and perfect power, so that no situation is beyond the scope of his power and nothing in heaven or earth can separate humanity from the love of God that is in Christ Jesus.

At this point, magnificently and movingly, the Lamb who is Christ, 'came and took the scroll from the right hand of him who sat on the throne'. Imagine it. The scroll is not offered to him. He takes it. The eyes of all creation are upon Christ as with authority he takes the scroll. He alone has the power to break open the seven seals that make the meaning of Life a closed book to us. Having broken the seals, he alone can show us what the riddle means. It is a spine-tingling moment. Creation holds its breath. There is a silence that can be felt.

---

8 G. B. Caird, *The Revelation of St John the Divine, Black's New Testament Commentaries*, London, Adam and Charles Black, 1966, p. 73.

And then all heaven breaks loose. There is an explosion of praise, wonder, worship, singing, shouts of acclamation. The noise is deafening. They sing a new song, because what is happening now has never happened before, and only a new song will do.

THE WORSHIP OF HEAVEN

Listen to the worship of heaven. The four living creatures and the twenty-four elders break out into praise, singing of a new community made up of every tribe and language and people and nation, a community given the unbelievable dignity of being kings and priests. Each creature and elder holds golden bowls full of incense, *which are the prayers of the saints*. In this aside, John affirms that no prayer is ever lost or falls out of reckoning. Every prayer ever spoken, in calm and turmoil, thoughtfully and quietly, in distress and panic, from great saints of God and lowly sinners, those repeated countless times and those cried out in the split second before the impact, every prayer is gathered up and brought into the presence of The Lamb.

And then the angels join in the great chorus, ten thousand times ten thousand of them and myriads more. The multitude of the heavenly host that sang on Christmas night, now see the ending of that part of the story. No wonder that they cry aloud (5:12):

Worthy is the Lamb, who was slain,
to receive power and wealth and wisdom and strength
and honour and glory and praise!

Even now John has not finished with us: 'Then I heard every creature in heaven and on earth and under the earth and on the sea ...' The whole of the created universe joins in the new song (5:13):

141

To him who sits on the throne and to the Lamb
be praise and honour and glory and power,
for ever and ever!

ENTERING THE VISION

The vision is not intended merely to tickle our fancy. We
began by recalling how we often feel a need to locate ourselves
somewhere. The main question to be asked in the light of
John's vision is 'Where are you standing as this picture
unfolds? Where do you locate yourself?' It is easy to view the
great spectacle on a screen, like the opening ceremony of the
Olympics or trooping the colour. But this is to take on the role
of a spectator.

The alternative is to move into the picture and find your-
selves taken up into it. Imagine the picture starting to curve
round and behind us, hearing it in Surround Sound. Then we
become a participant and not a spectator. The question this
movement into the picture provokes is a searching one: Is this
great vision the vision by which we live? It is a comprehensive
and coherent vision, which gives us infinite value, provides us
with purpose and direction and offers a future bright with
hope. One of the ways of defining what it is to be a Christian is
to say that it is someone who enters and lives in this Christ-
centred vision of the world. To put it more starkly, 'Are we
singing?'

Praise is a statement about the way things are, about who is
supremely valuable. Praise puts us exactly in the right location. Neither too low ('I am but a worm and can do nothing and
have nothing and am lower than nothing'), nor too high,
behaving like God and arrogating to myself that authority that
belongs rightly to God. It is not flattering God. It comes from a
heart deeply thankful for all that he has done in Christ and
that wants to register and recognize his supreme worth. Praise
frees me from looking at myself and from endless self-analysis
or self-aggrandisement.

RENEWING THE VISION

We need to keep the vision bright and fresh. Over the years Christians have developed hundreds of ways of doing this. Because it is a comprehensive vision, a world-view, it is like a web. This means that to tug on any part of it is to feel the pull of the whole. Picking out just the bits we like signifies a failure to understand that the vision is a map of absolutely everything there is.

As we hear the scriptures we enter into the story from Alpha to Omega. When we recite the creed we restate its truths. Stained-glass windows were made to keep the vision before the gaze of the faithful. Great Rose windows, designed to be a contradiction of the image of the wheel of Fate, remind us that Christ is at the centre of all things and we journey towards him. The shape of churches and cathedrals invites us to act out our walk from west window to the east, seeing ourselves moving within the outline of the cross. Icons freeze-frame the truth of the gospel in one moment, using a coded language of colour and reverse perspective, which we can learn. By cribs and Easter gardens, by banners and flowers, by the shape of the church's year – from Advent through Christmas and Easter to Pentecost and the season of the Kingdom, we renew the vision by which we live. Sometimes we may embody its truth in actions – kneeling, standing with arms uplifted, making the sign of the cross, closing the eyes, holding out empty hands, beating the breast, breaking bread, shaking hands.

For the John who wrote Revelation praise was clearly the primary way in which the worship of God and the vision of his glory was to be expressed. All Christian traditions emphasize its central role. The eucharistic prayers in the Church of England liturgy consist of a structured congregational act of praise, led by a President, but prayed by the whole congregation. The prayer rehearses the great story from creation to consummation by way of the narrative of the Last Supper and thanksgiving for the redemption we have in Christ. Despite variations in content, all the prayers echo the song of the four living creatures, the twenty-four elders, the hosts of angels and archangels and the whole of creation. More than one of the prayers ends with the very same words that are sung by every living creature in Revelation 5:13. So, here on earth, we join with everything that has breath. We add our weak words to theirs. But, if this is truly our vision, if we have entered into the picture and allowed it to envelop us, perhaps we ought to try to ensure that our weak words are as strong, triumphant, ecstatic, thankful, sincere, life-offering and jubilant as we can make them. If we sing them the sound should lift the roof, and the Amen, like that in heaven, should be deafening.

LIVING THE VISION

Heart-felt praise spills over into life. The hymn writer prays, 'Fill thou my life, O Lord my God, in every part with praise.' The vision is renewed in worship so that it can be lived out in the life of the week: 'Seven whole days, not one in seven, I will praise Thee.' Christians have always seen that daily work can be done to the glory of God and that anything, however menial or outwardly degrading, can be offered up as a sacrifice of praise and thanksgiving. Even on Monday morning as I drive to the soul-destroying office, the To Do list need not in fact destroy the soul. Everything can be offered to God, even those situations and responsibilities where I have little freedom or choice, where I am being pushed about by others. As daily work brings with it more and more stress, so learning to turn work into praise becomes more and more important. Under extreme pressure, driven to meet irrational targets, subject to unreasonable demands, called to meet unrelenting deadlines, working with impossible colleagues, the harassed Christian can still take time out to join the heavenly choirs. It is an amazing and transforming insight that says even the hardest parts of life can be offered to God as part of the offering of Praise.

This is a vision of life, of the whole of life, and it is a good vision. It unveils the nature of reality, the way things really are. It puts God – not the boss, nor money, nor myself, nor a random activity of nature – on the throne. It gives me value and worth. It offers purpose and direction and meaning. Within this vision millions of people down the ages have lived and been content to die.

REFLECTION

What experiences within the last few months have made you reflect upon the purpose of life?

What exactly might it mean for you to make the details of your daily life a sacrifice of praise and thanksgiving?

How is the concept of Christ as the key to life's meaning expressed in Christian art, hymnody and architecture?

DISCUSSION

Give examples of how ultimate questions about the meaning of life surface in ordinary conversation or on television programmes

In what ways do people without Christian faith give significance to life and their humanity?

As an act of worship, talk about and play pieces of music that evoke the praise of heaven.

PRAYER

Holy, holy, holy
Is the Lord God Almighty,
Who was, and is, and is to come.

You are worthy, our Lord and God,
To receive glory and honour and power,
For you created all things,
And by your will they were created and have their being.

Worthy is the Lamb who was slain,
To receive power and wealth and wisdom and strength,
And honour and glory and praise.

To him who sits upon the throne
And to the Lamb
Be praise and honour and glory and power,
for ever and ever.

CHAPTER 9

THE OBEDIENT SON

Spare a thought for the oniomaniacs. My dictionary doesn't contain the term but, apparently, it comes from a Classical Greek word for buying. We probably know them better as shopaholics. Research has shown that one in five women and one in ten men have problems with over-shopping. The irresistible urge to buy things leads a worryingly large number of people into credit card problems, serious debt, and at its worst, depression and even divorce. Christmas is a particularly perilous time for the shopaholic. Jane Gordon comments, 'For those of us who use retail therapy to boost serotonin levels in the brain ... Christmas is like happy hour for alcoholics.'[1]

It's customary to treat over-shopping as a bit of a joke. Imelda Marcos may need thirty thousand pairs of shoes but that's not our problem. When we feel down nothing perks us up quite so quickly as a visit to Bluewater or the Metro Centre. We call it 'retail therapy' and confess our sins with the same merry laugh we use for eating too much Black Forest gateau. But we have learned to take comfort-eating seriously. We no longer find it as uproariously droll as we used to. In its own way, comfort-buying may be just as emotionally damaging and financially much more destructive unless your appetite for gateaux is gargantuan.

What is going on here? Why has buying things acquired such prominence within our culture? The sociologists point out that at some time during the 1980s consumption gave birth to a baby called consumerism. Consumption is the purchase and use of goods and has been around since we stopped paying with chickens and goats for things we wanted.

---

1 Jane Gordon, ''Tis the season to be jolly careful – if you're an oniomaniac, that is', *Times* 2, 29 November 2000, pp. 4–5.

But consumerism is a view of the world, a perspective, a way of seeing life. By a mysterious process, the commodity, the thing we were buying, the object of consumption, gradually began to take on some form of magical quality. Sociologist Steven Miles observes that this process has been so widespread and so irresistible that 'Consumerism is *the* religion of the late twentieth century.'[2] Now anything that can seriously be called *the* religion of the twentieth century is of intense interest to the Christian.

The Consumerist Perspective

What are the key features of consumerism as a way of life? I think we can identify at least four.

Identity

Who I am is formed by what I buy and own. The individual's persona is made up of his or her shoes, clothes, car, camera, Walkman, television, video and a dozen other status-loaded, significantly symbolic possessions. Recently I sat in amazement through an advertisement for mobile phones. It seemed to go on for ten minutes and contained the memorable line 'We have just the one tailored to your individual needs.' I thought, 'For heaven's sake, it's a phone! It's a phone! One of those black bakelite things that used to sit in the hallway.' But that only goes to show how detached I am from the action. The mobile is not a phone; it's an extension of my personality, giving off as vital a message about who I am as the drink I order or the CDs I buy. Owning the high-status commodity is heavy with significance. Playstation2 was so deeply desired by so many people that the stocks sold out in one day as soon as they were available. The head of Sony Europe, no doubt trying to make it up to the thousands of British customers who were disappointed, announced, a touch pretentiously, 'Many

---

2 Steven Miles, *Consumerism – as a Way of Life*, London, Sage, 1998, p. 1.

elements of the game were developed in the UK. The UK can be proud of its place in the heritage of gaming.' The fashion pages of one of the national newspapers runs a regular feature called 'Get the look for less'. The logic seems to be 'Look at what is being worn on the catwalk. Now despair because you cannot possibly afford that stuff. But turn to page fifteen and you will find something less expensive that will still enable you to be Kate Moss or Naomi Campbell in your own street.' Image and identity come together. They are so closely connected that small boys are mugged by slightly bigger boys for their jackets, their jeans, their trainers, their mobiles and their shades. Consumerism shapes our identity. If we were looking for a slogan then it might be the witty parody of Descartes, *Tesco ergo sum* – I shop therefore I am.

Fulfilment

The second assumption made by the consumerist is that personal growth and fulfilment come by satisfying needs. The sequence of reasoning goes as follows: 'If I want it I probably need it'; 'If I need it I ought to have it'; 'If I ought to have it I must have it'; 'If I must have it I must have it now.' The characteristic behaviour of a vital human being is buying things. Acquisition is the mark of a life lived authentically. This principle assumes that the source of my life is to be found in my possessions. Every few years the megastar Elton John has a complete clear-out of his wardrobes. The last time this happened, hundreds of thousands of pounds worth of clothes came on to the market and were snapped up by admirers. Elton John admitted engagingly, 'I like buying things. And I like getting rid of them so that I've got room to buy the same amount of stuff again.' When I was young, I remember a neighbour saying to my mother, 'Oh, I don't think I could go on living without my cut glass.' Consumerism makes acquisition the keynote of life, the touchstone of success and the means of personal fulfilment. Its slogan is 'Go on, spoil yourself'.

Control

The attractiveness of this life is that it seems to offer people control over what they do. This is the third key feature of consumerism, and it has to do with power. Money does buy you a superior lifestyle. No one can order you around. Through the purchasing power of wealth and through the symbolic power of possessions I announce to the world and myself, 'I consume things. I gobble things up. And possibly I eat people.' The key word is customer *demand*. It is a demanding style of life, as evidenced by the strap lines in the advertisements: 'You're in charge', 'It's your call', 'You decide', 'You're at the wheel', 'What she wants she gets'. 'Don't mess with me' is the message of the advertisement that depicts a woman hand-cuffing her partner to the banisters because he dared borrow her car. The voice-over warns, 'Next time, ask before you borrow it.' The subliminal appeal is to the kind of confident woman who kicks sand in men's faces on the beach and does the stunts for *Charlie's Angels*. But the message tacitly includes both sexes; we'd all like to be that kind of assertive character. Wealth equals possessions equals control. Control through consumption means that you are accorded respect. My favourite example of sucking up to the customer with money to spend is the label on the complimentary packet of sweets received by guests checking in at The Beach House in Bal Harbour, Miami. It reads, 'You are courageous under circumstances of adversity and equally courageous when faced with your own success. The praise of others is irrelevant to you, and self satisfaction is unknown. You behold a mountain and ask only what lies beyond. We are honoured to have you sleep under our roof.'[3] The consumerist lifestyle promises that you will be in charge of your life and no one will push you around. The image that comes to mind is the mayhem that breaks out at the January Sales and the slogan, the peremptory and uncompromising 'Gotta have it'.

---

3 'Pretentious, Moi?', *Times 2*, 21 November 2000, p. 8.

Choice

Choice is primary in the appeal of consumerism. The consumer world typically offers a wide range of options in order to allow the customer the freedom to choose one and reject others. This often means that manufacturers introduce minor and irrelevant differences within a particular category of commodity in order to offer a range of options. Jeans are probably much of a muchness, and one version not much more comfortable or hard wearing than another, but a variety of labels allows choice among customers. Studies of the way in which Walkmans have been continuously redesigned and repackaged show Sony targeting different types of consumer through different shapes and designs of Walkman. Now the Walkman is available in over 700 different versions across the world. This range of options allows individuals to reinvent themselves, to mould their own present and future by taking what they want. There is a strong emphasis on autonomy, so that they are a law to themselves and in a continuing process of self-creation. A reviewer commented on a television documentary on contemporary life, 'Dominic and Bianca don't have a life; they have something called a lifestyle.' If we were looking for a slogan to sum up this aspect of consumerism it might be 'Feel free to shop around'.

CHRISTIANITY AS SHOPPING

I want to emphasize that in the preceding section I am not primarily criticizing shopping or consumption *per se* or the acquisition of possessions. Consumption is a necessary part of modern life. I neither have to milk the goat every morning nor bake my own bread nor weave my own clothes, though I suspect I would be a better man if I did. Nor am I wishing to attack materialism nor expose the devious tricks of marketing nor put in a plea for simplicity of lifestyle. I actually like shopping. I am more interested in consumerism as a way of living and a way of being me. The consumerist mindset, consumerist assumptions about the world and human values can shape and colour other aspects of our lives that appear to have nothing to do with shops or credit cards.

For example, you can view *friendship as shopping*. The consumer approach to friendship acquires friends who will be useful. Once acquired they can be used and manipulated. Behaviour like this pushes the concept of friendship to the limit. In fact, it can hardly qualify as friendship since the other person is no more than a commodity to be used and then discarded. 'You treat me like an object' is a clear sign that the other person has noticed what is going on. Yet it is extraordinary how long a relationship can drag on even when both parties have come to realize that there is more consuming than sharing going on.

Similarly, there is a consumerist style of sexuality. The promiscuous lifestyle collects notches on the bedpost but is unconcerned about commitment or vulnerability. This is *sex as shopping*. It focuses on acquisition, enjoyment and disposal. The consumer goes the rounds with a shopping list, looking for customer satisfaction. And, pretty much like filling up at a petrol station, he or she expects the transaction to be efficient, personally undemanding and to keep them going until the tank is empty again and needs to be refilled.

Unfortunately, it is also possible to find the consumerist mentality seeping into our understanding of the life of faith. This is *religion as shopping* and it goes something like this: When we ask what is the point of the Christian life, or why we should be Christians at all, it is easy to reply, 'To fulfil my needs.' The grace of God in salvation is directed entirely towards my personal safety and satisfaction. It is only a short step from that position to 'If I don't get what I pray for I shall switch brands' and 'If worship at this church doesn't meet my perceived needs I shall shop around.'

Or we might note the way Christianity can function as a divine insurance policy: 'I expect to be kept safe from every kind of harm. I don't expect to catch anything nasty or lose my friends through illness or accident. If something unpleasant does happen to me, I shall file a customer complaint and ask, politely but firmly, "God, what do you think you're playing at?" After all, where there's blame there's a claim.'

This mindset can affect our presentation of the gospel. The good news can be turned into a five-minute sales pitch, promising wonderful rewards in return for a quick confession of sin. Salvation as this year's star offer sits uneasily with a master who spoke of the narrow gate and the eye of the needle. Repentance is more than regret or remorse; it entails nothing less than the whole of life, turned round and inside out. The consumerist gospel of cheap grace sounds like 'treasure on earth and treasure in heaven'. Now that's what I call a bargain.

Sometimes we hear descriptions of gifts that make them sound more like instruments of power than ways of building up the body of Christ or serving others: 'I receive these gifts in order that I may enjoy a fulfilled life. I seldom, if ever, think about or pray for gifts like patience and endurance. The victorious life is up, up, up.'

We may have problems with the idea of total demand. 'No other gods' leaves no margin for error. 'A jealous God' sounds no more appealing than 'a jealous husband' or 'a jealous wife'. Can God seriously expect me to give him undivided allegiance? Customer loyalty is all very well, but he can't blame me for shopping at a few other shops if he doesn't seem to stock what I want.

God's Shopping Mall

Such a list is so uncompromisingly centred on the self that we quickly recognize it as wild exaggeration. I realize that few of us would say this kind of thing publicly or without embarrassment. We know that the above list is a caricature of faith and that this is not normally the way it is between God and ourselves. In any case I do not want to rule out entirely complaining at God. We have all found at times that expressing our grievances may be the way to a deeper experience of his love. We suspect, correctly, that God prefers honesty, even in the form of complaint, to mealy mouthed politeness.

Nevertheless, despite these proper qualifications, it may be a different story at the level of the emotions. At that level it is perfectly possible to feel as if God runs the universe like an enormous shopping mall for our benefit. And from time to time we catch ourselves talking and acting as if this were so. At such moments it may be reassuring to discover that the consumerist attitude was well known to the biblical writers.

The book of Job begins with the debate between God and Satan about the upright, God-fearing pillar of society who is Job. Satan asks the suspicious question, 'Does Job fear God for nothing?' The assumption is, 'Of course not. Like everyone else, Job is in it for what he can get out of it.' Satan's suggestion assumes the consumerist motive: 'Try a little unpleasantness and Job will stop serving you. He will switch to another brand. You will soon discover that there is no customer loyalty there.'

The Acts of the Apostles (Acts 8:9–25) contains a revealing incident involving a sorcerer named Simon. He has established himself in Samaria and has acquired a large following. He professes the Christian faith after hearing the preaching of Philip. Peter and John arrive in Samaria to confirm the work of Philip. They pray for the new converts and lay hands on them. They in their turn receive the Holy Spirit. This must have involved some kind of visible manifestation because Simon notices what has happened. The passage continues, 'When Simon saw that the Spirit was given at the laying on of the apostles' hands, he offered them money and said, "Give me also this ability so that everyone on whom I lay my hands may receive the Holy Spirit."' Once again we observe that consumerism is about control and the satisfaction of wants.

Other passages involve the disciples. In Mark 10:35–45, James and John take Jesus aside and ask for the seats on either side of Jesus in his glory. The rationale is 'Give us the seats either side of you. Surely we've earned them. We have followed you now for some time. We have priority booking.

After all, there's no point following you if it doesn't pay out somehow.' A decent place in heaven is the least you can expect for long-term customer loyalty.

In the same vein Peter (Mark 10:28) watches a rich man walk away from Jesus (in consumer terms, the cost of the product was higher than he was prepared to pay) and asks plaintively, 'We have left everything to follow you!' We all hear the unspoken follow-up question 'So, what do we get?'

These passages show that the consumerist element in the life of faith is nothing new. The motif lies at the heart of what it is to live as a Christian. I must emphasize again that the discussion is not primarily about shopping. It touches our motives for being Christians, our expectations and desires, our friendship with God and even our understanding of what it is to live an authentic human life. How do we follow Christ without turning every prayer into a shopping list and every good deed into a deposit against our loyalty card? There may be many people who will read this and wonder what on earth the fuss is about. For them none of this is a problem. I have a feeling, however, that the consumerist attitude to discipleship goes deeper and is more widespread and influential than we suspect.

THE BELOVED SON: LIVING LIFE GOD'S WAY

Like a breath of fresh air, we turn to Jesus as the model of one who follows the path of true discipleship, the Son who knows the Father, the perfect example of how to live the life of faith in God's way. His life is a contradiction of the consumerist perspective. The story of Christ's temptations (Matthew 4:1–11) is a paradigm of engaging with the key issues and resolving them through trust and obedience. In the crisis of Jesus wrestling with the tempter we see each feature of the consumerist creed explicitly denied.

Identity

Where is the source of Jesus' identity, his understanding of himself? It is clearly not derived from objects or possessions. Jesus frames his identity in terms of sonship. He is son to God as father. This understanding is shaped and confirmed by his experience at the river Jordan. At his baptism he hears the voice of the Father saying, 'You are my son. I love you. I am pleased with you. You are my delight.' Living out of that experience Jesus is able to fast for forty days in the wilderness. He is secure enough in the Father's love not to need to comfort eat. His identity is not something for which he must strive, but is a gift he has received.

Christians sometimes forget the power of their baptism remembered and brought into the present. At baptism God says, 'I love you. You are my beloved child. This is your identity. Do not allow anyone or anything to persuade you that you are less than immortal diamond.' This is even more dramatically represented in those Christian traditions that baptize infants. Children do very little at their baptism – the odd whimper or lusty bawl; perhaps a cry of ecstasy or an ambiguous noise from below. The rite emphasizes the truth that God shows his love for the child before he or she can speak. At a point when he or she knows nothing about God, the child is marked by the sign of the cross and is washed in the waters of baptism. To be a child of God does not depend on anything done or achieved. God's love comes as a gift.

Perhaps we do not rehearse enough the truth that God looks on us with delight. Part of the Christian nurture of children ought to include reminding them of their baptism in a variety of ways: 'You are a child of God. He loves you and thinks you are special. He will never stop loving you. He likes you. He thinks you are fantastic. And by the way, so do we.' Nor is remembering baptism just something we do for children. We need to do it for ourselves. Luther was fond of saying at critical points in his life, 'I have been baptized.'

Along with baptism go all those other experiences of the love of God, whether in worship or prayer, in walking the hills or sitting quietly in a country church. Return to them again and again. Keep them fresh in the memory. You are precious to God. You do not have to earn his love. We each have our own particular moments at the Jordan. In the strength of those experiences we can go forty days in the desert.

Fulfilment

What is the key to personal fulfilment according to the temptation narratives? How do we grow as persons? The satanic answer is that it comes by having what you want when you want it. 'If you're hungry, make loaves. Where's the problem?' I'm not sure that there would have been anything particularly wrong about Jesus breaking his fast. The decision to fast was presumably a personal one, taken in order that he should be able to concentrate on his relationship with his Father and work through the implications of the baptism experience. Therefore, he could break the fast whenever it suited him. But *in the context*, using his powers to gratify this desire took on a significance far beyond the actual decision to resume eating. It became one of those critical moments when the issue of what is most important to you in life is suddenly at stake. Of course he must eat, and bread, however produced, is a gift from God. But in this temptation a dilemma is made concrete, embodied in a specific decision.

Eating or not eating, making loaves or continuing to feed on the presence of God becomes a field test of Jesus' whole outlook on how to live life to the full. The question is posed, 'Where is the source of your life to be found?' We all know of moments that seem heavy with significance. Issues we have wrestled with in our heads are suddenly laid out in front of us, distilled and embodied in a specific choice. And the decision to speak or stay silent, to act or refrain from acting, to lie or speak a difficult truth, can carry our whole life within it. 'Are you one of his disciples?' – such an innocent question – tore Peter apart at the trial of Jesus. To the bystander the inquiry and the answer was of little interest. Peter knew it went to the heart of his proud claim 'Lord, we have left all to follow you.' Jesus' reply to the tempter shows that he stands on the truth that we are truly brought to life not by the physical and material but by the word of God. So he turns from 'Go on, spoil yourself' to friendship with the Father. 'I live and find my fulfilment in feeding on the words that come from God. That's where I find nourishment and life.'

Control

'Throw yourself off the pinnacle; God will catch you' portrays God as a divine all-risks insurance policy. A comprehensive insurance policy as it turns out, since the small print of the psalm Satan quotes covers even Acts of God (Psalm 91:9–13). But Jesus refuses the temptation. What is going on here? I cannot see that Satan is misquoting scripture, although this is sometimes claimed. The psalm is remarkably clear: 'He will command his angels to guard you in all your ways; they will lift you up in their hands, so that you will not strike your foot against a stone.' It looks as if it means what it says. Why shouldn't Jesus jump? After all, Psalm 91 invites him to trust God.

Except, of course, that trusting God is not quite what is at stake. The background to Jesus' answer – you shall not put God to the test – is Israel's murmuring in the wilderness. The people began to complain that God was not with them and decided to test the relationship. 'The day of provocation' as it came to be called was an attempt to force God's hand, to coerce God into doing something because they wanted it so. Essentially it was an attempt to control God. Now we can see why Jesus refused to jump. Externally, there is no visible difference between a leap of faith and a leap of provocation. The observer sees only a falling body. But from the inside Jesus knows that his leap would have been provoking God, manipulating him by forcing his hand. It would be the equivalent of a child trying to manoeuvre a parent to do what they want with the words 'You've said it and now you *must* do it.' I sometimes wonder what would have happened if Jesus had jumped. I imagine God catching him but saying sadly, as he sets him

gently down on the ground, 'I promised to catch you and so I
have. But something precious between us has been destroyed.'
In the event Jesus rejects 'Gotta have it': the relationship with
the Father is a fragile and delicate thing, not to be abused.

Choice

The third temptation offers glory, status and power, those
eminently desirable commodities, but at a price. It is not
likely that Satan was suggesting that Jesus should switch allegiances. The choice seldom comes in that stark form. The test
is a more familiar and less shocking one. Glory, status and
power come at a modest cost. Satan merely asks, reasonably,
that Jesus divide his loyalties. 'Give some allegiance to God
and some to other values, such as those I represent.' We can
feel the force of the suggestion. After all, isn't there something
extreme, even fanatical about having only one focus, one
allegiance? Total commitment, undivided loyalty, smacks
of intolerance, even a kind of intellectual fascism. It's also
imprudent. You need to spread your investment portfolio
across a range of companies. Putting all your eggs in one
basket is bad business and bad religion. What if God goes bust?

Jesus' answer is uncompromising. God alone is the centre of
my life. Later in his ministry he will say that you cannot serve
two masters and that the only safe thing to do with Money is
to get it off your hands as fast as possible, before its tentacles
wind themselves around your heart. Later he will say that he
has come to set a man against his son and a daughter against
her mother. Later he can demand that his followers put their
hands to the plough and do not look back. He can say these
things because here in the desert the crucial battle has been
fought and won. God is the supreme value in human life. So
Jesus says no to every temptation to compromise or dilute his
commitment. Shop around to see if there is a better deal to be
had? Never.

Freedom and Dissatisfaction

Here are two ways of living that stand in stark contrast. The consumerist lifestyle and the life of faith contradict each other. In concluding this chapter I want to address two questions raised by setting the two ways side by side.

Where Is Freedom to Be Found?

At first sight the answer is straightforward. The consumer lifestyle looks like freedom and autonomy. The life of faith looks like slavery and constraint. Apparently, the favourite song at funerals is 'I did it my way' – it suggests independence and just the right amount of nonchalance about the wishes of others. By contrast, it is easy to caricature the life of faith as an emotional crutch clasped by feeble inadequates unwilling to take the risk of making up their own minds and frightened of freedom.

In fact, the reverse is true. The freedom and choice of consumerism is largely an illusion. Those who offer it make sure that it is restricted. We know that big business creates demand and controls choice. 'Give the public what they want' is fine as a principle, provided you have already latched on to the best way of convincing the public that *this* is what they want. I remember my surprise when a senior executive of a large company told me, 'Our job is not to provide a service or supply a product but to create a customer.' Of course he was right but, in my innocence, I had never seen it before. I should have noticed that football clubs change their away strips regularly in order to force parents to buy replacement kit for their children. Brand loyalty has to be carefully constructed – usually covertly, on our behalf by those who know best and 'for our own good'. The artificial creation of pop groups for a specific segment of the market is hardly a new phenomenon, though examples seem to have multiplied recently. They demonstrate the fact that we do not choose our musical tastes freely. But then, it's likely that we do not choose our food, drink or clothes freely either. The consumerist lifestyle is a driven life.

Paradoxically, a relationship with firm commitments allows freedom. The apparent restrictions of the marriage vows give security and allow freedom for growth. 'I take you, to have and to hold, for better for worse, for richer for poorer, in sickness and in health, till death us do part' sounds like a life sentence. But within such an exclusive relationship many decisions are made in advance of the need to make them. They do not need to be agonized over, since the nature of the commitment rules out certain courses of action. For example, neither partner is available for adultery. Lived out responsibly, the promises put the marriage on a different basis from purely physical attraction or sexual performance. Within those limits it is possible for both husband and wife to enjoy security, to be relaxed and natural in the presence of the opposite sex, to grow old without anxiety about their orgasm rating and within the framework of a shared life, of bed and board, to have the time and space to get to know each other at depth.

Artists speak of the *discipline* of the art form or of the material. You can only do certain things with wood or stone or a moving body or a sonnet form. A dance that involves pirouetting unaided on one finger cannot be danced in this universe. A sonnet cannot have 49 lines. But within the discipline of the form or the material there is freedom to be found. To have no limits does not normally mean greater freedom. It tends towards the loss of the *pressure*, that constraint, that produces the work of art.

Not everyone accepts the wisdom of this principle of freedom through constraints, particularly when it is applied to Christianity. The prayer may speak of a 'service which is perfect freedom' but many would still assume that commitment and obedience to God spell the death of freedom. When the Galilean conquers, the world grows grey at his breath. A prominent humanist puts the case forcefully:

But the Christian must remain concentrated upon and bound by the example of Christ as the supreme model for human living. Now Christ as a human personality is an enigma, but as a standard and pattern there is no doubt or obscurity about him: he is the archetype of unqualified submission and obedience to the will of God, the God of Abraham and of Isaac and of Jacob. It is impossible to follow Christ on any other terms, and the humanist finds acceptance of these terms a violation of himself and his whole experience. His rejection of Christ is therefore categorical: he can do no other.[4]

There is not much to add to what has already been said. In this quotation we encounter the clash of two opposing ways of living. For those who are convinced that following Christ is a violation of themselves, I can only say, 'Then you have never tried it.' Let Jesus have the last word: 'If the son shall set you free you shall be free indeed.'

How Do you Cope with Disappointment?

Deficit, falling short, lack, scarcity, disappointment, dissatis-faction – whatever it's called – the experience of *not having* is a major problem for the consumer. Failure to possess is a primary cause of the frustration that leads to theft. The myths of our society, typified in the television show *Who Wants to Be a Millionaire?*, teach us that wealth is possible for anyone. We form the impression that everyone is winning millions on the National Lottery. 'It could be you' and though it probably won't be, given the odds, you're not to know that and some-body's got to win.

The corollary of this message is that if you *don't* have, you are little by little becoming a non-person. What happens when the cupboard is bare and you have nothing to consume? Failure to achieve or acquire constitutes an attack on one's identity, loss of control over one's life, the reduction of options to one or, even worse, to none. However do you cope when life doesn't give you what you want? The Lottery sells dreams – so

---

4 H. J. Blackham, 'Humanism: the subject of the objections', in *Objections to Humanism*, H. J. Blackham (ed.), London, Constable, 1963, p. 18.

scratch the cards in hope – but an instant later the itch is still there.

The truth is that most of us will never have what we really, really want. The majority of people are dissatisfied with the body and personality they received when the genes were being shared out. We would like to be taller, shorter, leaner, blonder, darker. A little more bulk in the upper body for some, a little less pear-shaped for others. We'd also like to be brighter, richer, healthier and younger. The prospect of designer babies shows that for some, the dissatisfaction extends to those around them. Getting old feels like an infringement of our consumer rights. Ill health is not what was down in the game plan. The good life is defined in terms of success in every aspect of life.

Unfortunately, life is about coping with shortcomings, imperfections and deficiencies. For the consumerist, having to wait, in the sense of not being in charge, waiting for or waiting on someone else is not good news. Redundancy, illness, disability, loss are disasters. Having no power to change anything or affect outcomes is calamity. The message that you should learn to 'respond positively and faithfully to the endless difficulties of life is *a seed on stony ground*'.[5]

I read in the newspaper of Jill Miller's experience of giving birth to a Down's syndrome child. Forty years after the birth she writes, 'Catherine is her own ambassador. Full of love, she engenders love in other people ... The birth of a Down's syndrome baby is not a disaster. Catherine has taught me much – most of all she has taught me how to love.'[6] I am moved almost to tears by the sheer joy on the face of the winner of the women's 200 metres at the Paralympics. Suddenly I realize that the consumer universe bears as much relation to reality as the indoor shopping mall, with artificial trees and waterfalls of pumped water promising perpetual springtime.

5 R. W. L. Moberly, *The Bible, Theology and Faith*, Cambridge, Cambridge University Press, 2000, p. 240.
6 Jill Ashley Miller, 'She taught me to love', *Times* 2, 8 August 2000, p. 13.

Jesus takes by the throat the experiences of real life – hunger, poverty, lack, hardship, weariness, pain – and uses them to strengthen his friendship with God. *Human beings do not live by bread alone* is the secret of an authentic human life. Jesus opens up for us a way of living passionately in the real world. Lack and imperfection don't have to be disasters or catastrophes.

Real human living comes by giving your life away, not by holding on to everything and trying to get more. Jesus is not in it for what he can get out of it. And because he is not in it for what he can get out of it God gives him everything. At the end of Matthew's gospel, twenty-four chapters on from the Temptations, Jesus can say, 'All authority in heaven and on earth has been given to me' (28:18). God *gives* what it would have been wrong for Jesus to *take*.

We follow Christ because he is our joy and treasure – the pearl beyond price. The friendship with him is worth more than anything in the world. Therefore it must be guarded and cherished, never presumed upon or taken for granted. It requires of us the willingness to be still and listen, to take time to be with God, to obey his voice, and trust in his goodness, using the trials, the difficulties and disappointments of life to grow in the knowledge of his love.

REFLECTION

Your house is on fire. What do you want to dash in and save? What does that tell you about yourself?

Think of some times when you had to obey someone. How did you react? What were you saying inside?

What difference does it make if *God* asks for your obedience?

At what times in your life have you experienced the love of God and felt that he delights in you?

DISCUSSION

Some see the life of faith as 'If the son shall set you free, you shall be free indeed'; others as 'the world has grown grey at his breath'. Collect evidence for both sides of the debate.

In what ways, other than those mentioned in this chapter, can one view 'the Christian life as shopping'?

Share examples of people who have handled imperfection, deficiency and disaster in creative ways.

PRAYER

Abba, Father,

Surround me with your love,
Assure me that I am your beloved child,
Help me to hear you say, 'I delight in you'.

Source of my life, give me grace to feed on you,
Protector of my life, give me grace to trust in you,
Lord of my life, give me grace to choose you in all things.

For in serving you I shall find freedom.

CHAPTER 10

THE RADIANT FACE

Christianity has had its fair share of eccentrics. St Cuthbert spent all night up to his neck in the North Sea praying. Simeon Stylites sat in the desert on top of a pole and as weevils fell out of his bodily cavities he replaced them with the words 'Eat what God has given you'. The lice found crawling through the clothes of St Thomas à Becket were apparently proof of sanctity, not a distressing lack of personal hygiene. On any account this behaviour is seriously weird. What are we to make of it?

Beginning with the outside, with what is observable, is almost certainly starting in the wrong place. Many human activities are baffling when you meet them without the aid of a guide – American football and Friday night pub crawls to name only two. It is the heart of the matter, the purpose, intention or goal, that explains what is really going on.

For example, what reply would I get if I asked a range of people, 'Is there anything or anybody almost more important than life itself? Who or what is it that you long for with something akin to an ache, a deep, desperate yearning? Who or what dominates your waking and sleeping hours, your work and your play, and colours all your projects and plans?'

There have been some odd answers to these questions, among them, believe it or not, Liverpool Football club, Elvis Presley, Kylie Minogue, my collection of matchboxes and my prize marrows. It's surprising how many people try to get their ashes scattered on the pitch at Old Trafford. Occasionally the reply might fasten on a fantasy figure: the most wonderful man in the world, he of the dark, brooding eyes, the lean, muscular body. As the video shop owner said when *Pride and Prejudice* was first screened, 'It's wall-to-wall Darcy in here.'

More commonly, the answer will focus on a real person – my wife or husband, my children.

AT THE HEART OF THE MATTER

Once you know the centre of someone's life it is easier to make sense of their behaviour. For Christians the heart of their faith is *the beatific vision*, that is, to see the face of God. This is what religion is really about. Even bizarre practices look less peculiar when you see them as aspects of devotion to Christ. At its heart Christianity is not an elaborate insurance policy – with unreasonably high premiums. It is not a regime of moral workouts in the spiritual gym with disapproval of the slackers thrown in. Nor is it believing six impossible things before breakfast. Nor one of a hundred optional leisure interests, so that A goes to Mass while B is off to *Stretch and Tone*, X plays darts and Y speaks in tongues. At its heart it is about gazing on the face of God.

'Gazing on the face of God' – this kind of exalted language demands at least a moment's reflection. Is it true for you? Is it religious rhetoric? Christianity is rather good at overstating the case, getting drunk on words and letting poetry make do for serious and realistic self-examination. Is all this stuff about visions of bliss grossly sentimental? Even worse, does it lead to such high expectations that we are doomed to be let down? Can such feverish experiences be owned only by a few highly strung and over-emotional souls? And, to be absolutely prosaic and harshly realistic, is the experience of the love of God really better than going on living – not living at a temperature of 104 – but living ordinary, unexciting, moderately satisfying lives, lacking the spiritual Everests of the saints but none the less living? If I don't have hyper experiences, am I really missing so much?

WHERE THE SAINTS HAVE TROD

Even if we think like this we should still listen to the voices of the saints. We soon find that we are not short of examples.

Mary sits at the feet of Jesus and is praised for choosing a better role than that of her sister who is frenetically taken up with food preparation. Paul sets his past achievements alongside knowing Christ and reckons that, by comparison, everything else is dung (Philippians 3:4–10). The author of *The Cloud of Unknowing* speaks of 'being pierced with the longing dart of love'. Gerard Manley Hopkins prays, 'O thou Lord of life, send my roots rain'. A hymn echoes it, 'Thou, O Christ, art all I want, / freely let me drink of thee. / Spring thou up within my heart, / rise to all eternity.' In *Of the imitation of Christ*, one of the great spiritual classics, Thomas à Kempis puts it like this: 'Refresh thy hungry beggar, inflame my coldness with the fire of thy love, enlighten my blindness with the brightness of Thy presence ... Lift up my heart to Thee in Heaven and send me not away to wander over the earth. O that with thy presence thou wouldest wholly inflame, consume and transform me into thyself. Suffer me not to go away from thee hungry and dry.'

This is the heart of the matter and I could quote literally thousands of examples like these. Even though many of us would find it hard to write in this way, even harder to talk about it, and tiring to live at this level of intensity, yet we know that if we lose contact with this kind of experience we run the risk of inhabiting an empty shell. All Christians know periods of spiritual dryness, when faith is not much more than going through the motions – this is normal – but to go for year after year lacking all sense of the presence of Christ is a desperate state in which to find oneself. In this condition, faith feels empty and the soul is dry. The language of hymns and liturgy, of poets and mystics are empty of meaning. Worse still, the odour of play-acting forced upon those who have lost the passion for God is what people outside the church sniff when they find Christianity distasteful, hypocritical, trivial and constricting. It is Kierkegaard's 'sickness unto death'.

I am not suggesting that in this life we will do much more than catch glimpses of God from time to time. However, life with no glimpses, no deeper experience of him, sits awkwardly with Paul's references to seeing the face of Christ, being filled with his fullness, knowing the love of Christ that is beyond knowledge and is joy unspeakable. A friend of mine likens it to driving in the Alps. Most of the time your eyes are fixed on the road – hairpin bends and precipitous drops have that effect. Suddenly you turn a corner and are confronted with a view that takes your breath away. Then it's back to the road again. But the vision stays with you.

Longing to see the face of God is a frequent motif in the writings of C. S. Lewis. In *The Pilgrim's Regress*, John, the central figure, catches a glimpse of an island at the far end of a wood. The vision brings with it unbounded sweetness and a piercing pang. And almost immediately it fades. The rest of John's life is spent trying to find the island:

> Among the hills of the western horizon, he thought that he saw a shining sea, and a faint shape of an Island, not much more than a cloud. It was nothing compared with what he had seen the first time: it was so much further away. But his mind was made up. That night he waited till his parents were asleep, and then, putting some few needments together, he stole out by the back door and set his face to the West to seek for the Island. [1]

St Paul was clear that the right place to see the glory of God was in the face of Jesus Christ (2 Corinthians 4:6). *We* are transformed as we look at his face; we also catch a glimpse of a transfigured *world*, the island of John's search. The world of the beatific vision is not an alien world. It is the world for which we were made. In seeking it, we fulfil the law of our being. This is authentic human living. We are not wandering aimlessly, but are on our way home.

---

1 C. S. Lewis, *The Pilgrim's Regress*, London, Geoffrey Bles, 1956, p. 32.

A World Charged with the Glory of God

Two passages in the New Testament show us the face of Christ in glory. One is the vision of the risen Christ in the book of Revelation; the other is the strange story of the Transfiguration, found in all three of the synoptic gospels (Matthew 17:1–8; Mark 9:2–8; Luke 9:28–36). There are minor variations between the accounts but I shall trace the story primarily through Luke's telling of it. The story raises a number of important questions: What is going on? What can it teach us about seeing the glory of God in the face of Jesus Christ? And, since the disciples' experience sounds like the kind of thing most of us want desperately, what do we have to do in order to have it?

So, first, what is going on? The episode gives the disciples little new information about Jesus. His messiahship has already been declared by Peter and his forthcoming death openly foretold by Jesus himself – even though not understood by the twelve (Luke 9:18–27). For eight chapters Luke's narrative has made it clear that Law and Prophets point to Jesus as the one who should come. If you ignore the disciples' obtuseness, the transfiguration offers nothing that has not already been stated. So how is it different from what has gone before?

In essence the disciples *see Jesus as he really is*. The curtain is drawn aside and they perceive 'his glory'. Matthew speaks of a face that shines like the sun and clothing as white as the light. Mark, a little heavy-footed, assures the readers that no laundry on earth could get clothes whiter. Luke struggles for words and comes up with 'the appearance of his face was ... well ... different' or 'other'. Indeed it was. It was the face of Jesus – of that there was no doubt – but a face that was *other* – transformed. The glory that was normally hidden from human gaze shone through.

I take it then that the story is as much about the disciples as it is about Christ. They see Jesus 'in a new light'. Half-formed impressions and tentative conclusions take on 'weight' or 'intensity', because, if I can put it this way, what has been only 'heard' up to this point, is now 'seen'. This experience gives a new 'depth' to the disciples' understanding.

We sometimes say, 'It was a complete revelation to me,' when we want to express the idea of old truths taking on a strange freshness. In those situations things we have taken for granted or have known in 'our heads' are suddenly rejiggled kaleidoscopically into a new arrangement. Then it seems as if a curtain has been drawn aside. Revelation is not an injection of extra facts; it is the creation of a new world.

Luke's portrayal of Jesus on the mountain comes laden with theological freight. But the way he tells the story stresses that the disciples *experienced* the theology rather than received it in their heads. They *see* the truth about Christ's person: in the close communion of prayer the veil between earth and heaven becomes wafer thin and his true glory shines through. They *see* how he fulfils the Scriptures: Moses the great prophet and giver of the law, and Elijah the one who will come immediately before 'the great and terrible day of the Lord' (Malachi 4:4) stand on the mountain with Jesus as his predecessor and his precursor. They *see* the meaning of the cross: the three figures talk together about a new Exodus from slavery. They *see* Jesus as the beloved Son: the cloud of God's presence comes down and physically envelopes them. Just as icons represent abstract truths in faces, gestures, colours and the arrangement of figures, so the transfiguration is theology 'embodied'.

Best of all, at the heart of their experience is one of those moments for which we all long – they see the king in his splendour and gaze upon his face. This is not the same thing as either ecstasy or mystical experience, though it may contain elements of both. I would prefer to emphasize the feeling that God has become real. An encounter with the living God brings with it the sense that I *have touched the rock*, been addressed by God, nourished in some deep part of my life, moved to adoration, silent contemplation or practical action.

Such an experience carries total conviction and transforms my perspective. Everything is transfigured – Christ, myself and my world. All look different in his light. Edwin Muir's poem *The Transfiguration* beautifully captures this idea of everything made new in Christ. He imagines that the vision of glory is a kind of restoration of Eden:

> The source of all our seeing rinsed and cleansed
> Till earth and light and water entering there
> Gave back to us the clear unfallen world.[2]

'The source of all our seeing rinsed and cleansed.' The experience is deep and transforming. Peter says as much: 'It is good for us to be here.'

Coming Down to Earth

The disciples do not want the vision to fade and Peter's words 'Let us put up three shelters' are a vain attempt to freeze the scene. Three booths made out of the sticks lying around at the top of the mountain do not amount to much, but we can understand that this moment of glory is such a taste of heaven that, in his position, we too might say anything to make it go on for ever.

In practice, such experiences don't come as often as we would like. Like the disciples, we must come down to earth. The gospel writers set the story within other passages designed to make sure we do not get above ourselves.

First, they make it clear that transfigurations cannot be timetabled; even if we want them very much, we cannot engineer their arrival. Jesus breaks in on the disciples' routine and decides he will take three of them away, privately, up on to the mountain. They do not ask for this and they do not control what will happen on the summit. It is Jesus who takes them out of ordinary time. I cannot switch on glimpses of glory or command that they happen at my say-so. In some mysterious

---

2 Edwin Muir, *Collected Poems*, London, Faber and Faber, 1960, pp. 198ff.

way this moment on the mountain is part of Christ's work in the lives of the three disciples. Neither they nor we can say exactly what he has in mind for them.

Secondly, the encounter with the shining face of Christ is not to be detached from the hard path of discipleship and the choices it involves. All the gospels link the transfiguration with Peter's confession at Caesarea Philippi and the first prediction of the passion. These episodes raise the stakes considerably; they force the theme of suffering into the conversation. Following Christ means losing one's life, not instant access to unlimited goodies. Stark choices are laid out. Being a disciple is not a matter of playing about, trying on a costume for size and style to see if it suits you. The transfiguration is not the equivalent of a spiritual sauna and jacuzzi.

Finally, the transfiguration experience is followed by a series of failures on the part of the same disciples who saw Jesus on the mountain. They are powerless to help an epileptic boy. They squabble about which disciple is the greatest. John stops an exorcist casting out demons because he is not one of Jesus' party and, together with his brother, helpfully offers to strike a Samaritan village with a thunderbolt, should Jesus be agreeable. This is the disciples at their most unlovely. We, like they, had better not suppose that glimpses of glory have to do with our sanctity. The disciples fail their Master even after they have been dazzled by his radiance.

Stay Here and Keep Watch with me

Nevertheless, though suitably chastened, we might still ask, 'But is there anything we *can* do to see the face of the king?'

The answer appears to be 'yes'. Put baldly, *the disciples stay awake*. This may seem a trivial point to make but let me expand it a little. It is clear that the disciples come to the mountain with all their frailty intact. They are not transformed; they remain boringly consistent. They are burdened with sleep – a code phrase for indicating obtuseness. Dozy disciples are prone to miss visions of the divine. In Gethsemane they sleep during the Lord's agony. And receive his sad reproof 'Could you not watch with me one hour?' Examples of their lack of insight abound in all the gospels. And yet, *they manage to stay awake*. And by so doing they do not miss the glory.

The Greek word translated 'having stayed awake' is *diagregoresantes*. Oddly enough, it has caused the translators a moderate amount of trouble. If you consult a range of Bibles, you will find that a surprising number are sure that the disciples fell asleep, almost missed the vision but woke up at the last minute. I am not sure why these translations are so coy. The most natural way to take Luke 9:32 is 'They were weighed down with sleep but, *having stayed awake*, they saw his glory.' Elsewhere in the New Testament the verb *gregoreo* is almost a technical term for keeping watch or vigil. 'Watch and pray' invites Christians to be alert and watchful not just 'awake' in the sense of not nodding off. 'Keep watch with me' is its sense. The straightforward way to take Luke's account is to suppose that the disciples were heavy with sleepiness but managed to 'watch through', keeping vigil with Jesus and thereby catching a sight of his glory.

The message is clear. On this occasion, the disciples behave in the style of Mark 13:5, where servants are commanded to watch actively for the master's return and make sure that they are not found sleeping when he comes. Moments of glory may come unbidden but they do not have to be unlooked for. It is our job to be awake to the possibility. This means watching out for the Master, keeping vigil with him in regular prayer and meditation, and taking advantage of times out of the routine of daily life. The disciples are witnesses – but only just. It is a tiny victory over the flesh. But it is enough.

JESUS WAS FOUND ALONE

Peter's suggestion to make up booths, like spare beds, is put firmly in its place by Luke's terse assessment that 'He did not know what he was talking about.' His offer will not be accepted. Suddenly we understand that Peter is not in control of this situation. It is beyond him. It is a mystery, bigger than he can grasp, resisting analysis. As the vision fades it leaves Peter tossed along in the torrent of the love and glory of God, trying to put his feet down but not able to touch the bottom, not knowing what is happening but wanting it all to last for ever. It will not be the last time that a follower of Christ will find that words will not do; nor that his or her attempts to control the situation will prove grossly inadequate. Peter needs to stop talking and trying to be helpful. One day he will learn to let God manage the script.

As Peter speaks, the cloud, which is the visible presence of God, envelops them. The vision fades; in their terror the disciples are left with a bare word: 'This is my son, my chosen one. *Listen to him*.' He is the Living Word. It is the words of Jesus that bring life and nourish the soul. They have the power to shape a soul, to bring healing and forgiveness, to unveil the meaning of life, to set people on their feet, to call them to great tasks, to heal the deepest hurts and to offer hope in place of despair. Everything the disciples saw on the mountain is now focused on the importance of listening to Jesus and learning to find the source of their life not in bread alone, 'but by every word that proceeds from the mouth of God'.

Thus the experience remains uncompromisingly centred on Christ. It is not to be confused with warm but vague feelings, or cosmic consciousness, or of being one with everything there is, or spooky shudders and awesome dread. It was not provided to give them 'meaningful memories of special times' but to command their devotion and obedience. The voice of God points the disciples' attention to Jesus – the beloved son and suffering servant. As the vision fades and the cloud disappears it is the Jesus with whom they had spent three years who draws near, touches them and tells them not to be afraid. 'When the voice had spoken, they found that Jesus was alone' (Luke 9:36). They are left with Jesus. Why would they want anyone else? Christian devotion is devotion to Christ.

BEYOND THE SACRED PAGE

How, in practical terms, do we keep watch and stay awake for the transforming moment? The words from the cloud direct us towards listening to Christ. Heeding his words and seeing his face are two sides of the same coin. If we take time to do one, we may experience the other. And where are Christ's words to be found? The answer of Christian spirituality down the years has been 'in the written word of the scriptures'.

Christians of different centuries and of very different traditions are unanimous on this. Christ is to be found in the reading of the Bible. Archbishop Mariano Magrassi's introduction to a method known as *lectio divina* contains a vast number of examples of how the Fathers of the church viewed the scriptures. In his collection we discover that reading them is an 'anticipation of divine glory' or 'a kiss of eternity'. Godfrey of Admont says, 'Sacred scripture is the breast of Jesus.' To open the scriptures is to set off on a search for the beloved, so that it is less a matter of reading a book as of seeking a person. Honorius in his commentary on the Song of Songs declares, 'With all its ardour, the church seeks in scripture the One whom she loves.' What is particularly interesting about this collection is Magrassi's conclusion: 'The ancients insisted especially on the link between scripture and the beatific vision.'[3]

Such a view of the scriptures does not imply that the insights and approaches of biblical scholarship are to be jettisoned. However, it does emphasize a different purpose in

---

3 Archbishop Mariano Magrassi, *Praying the Bible: An Introduction to Lectio Divina* (tr. Edward Hagman), Minnesota, The Liturgical Press, 1998, p. 24.

reading. The desire to meet Christ in the scriptures is central. For Augustine, desire is the key ingredient: 'Give me a lover, he will feel that of which I speak: in this wilderness, sighing for the springs of his eternal homeland: give me such a man, he will know what I mean.'[4]

We come with this desire to the mountain hoping to see the face of Christ. What practical wisdom is available to us? I begin with a word about process. The busy work of the intellect properly involved in much theological study is less appropriate for our purpose than unhurried reflection. The imagination and the heart are more engaged than analysis and reason; rather than looking to a product, we expect to end in prayer and adoration; if there are truths to be revealed we hope to see them in the face of Christ. I am reminded of Anthony de Mello's comment that 'No one ever became drunk on the *word* wine.'[5]

LECTIO DIVINA

From the fourth century onwards the method of Bible reading known as *lectio divina*, 'divine reading', or, more loosely, 'reading with God in mind' was widely used. A proper study of *lectio divina* is beyond the scope of this chapter but the name is less important than the process. As one might expect, reading the scriptures in this mode cannot be hurried. We cannot enter into a conversation with Christ in a perfunctory and demanding manner. We need to sit quietly and stop thinking about booth-building.

There are four movements in *lectio divina*: reading, meditation, prayer and contemplation. Magrassi quotes Guigo's summary: 'Reading, as it were, puts food whole into the mouth, meditation chews it and breaks it up, prayer extracts its

---

4 Augustine, *Tract. in Ioan.* 26.4.
5 Anthony de Mello, *The Song of the Bird*, New York, Doubleday, Image Books, 1984, p. 2.

flavour, contemplation is the sweetness itself which gladdens and refreshes.'⁶ As we begin reading, we choose a short passage from the Bible and read it slowly verse by verse, taking our time before moving on. This reading is attentive, unhurried and calm. It is helpful often to read the verses slowly and aloud, waiting for a phrase to 'bite'. Meditation begins when we are struck by a word or phrase and chewing it over, sometimes repeating it over and over again, allow it to do its own work in us. 'Ruminating' was the way the Fathers described it, but I like Esther de Waal's image of rocking a baby backwards and forwards.⁷ At some point the heart is touched and we are open to Christ. Prayer, the third stage, like conversation, will emerge naturally from the subject of the passage. Such prayer may take the form of thanksgiving, recollection, confession of sin or intercession for others. In time a sense of completion may come and the words of prayer will give way to sitting quietly in the presence of Christ. This stage is contemplation, sitting with Christ, not doing anything much, just being with him.

It is important not to be too purist about this process. What is being described is a possible method – a slow, reflective, prayerful reading of a small portion of the Bible. I think it works best with a passage that allows you to take one word or a short phrase or sentence. Sometimes such a word can go with you right through the day: 'Be still and know that I am God'; 'I am the way, the truth and the life'; 'my grace is sufficient for you, my strength is made perfect in weakness'. Phrases like these go deep and open us up to Christ's presence.

PLAYING WITH IMAGES

The sequence followed in *lectio divina* is a good one for any kind of reflection on scripture. A second kind of meditation

---

6 In Magrassi, *Praying the Bible*, p. 104.
7 Esther de Waal, *A Life-Giving Way*, London, Geoffrey Chapman, 1995, p. 142.

gives greater scope to the imagination. Here the images and pictures of the passage are the subject of our attention. Again, begin by reading slowly and attentively but pause when an image grips you. Now dwell in the picture and allow your imagination to play with it, fleshing out its different aspects, letting it evoke memories and feelings, making free connections with other aspects of your experience. In Jerome's words, 'unfurl your sails to the wind of the Holy Spirit'. This is not the same process used by those who receive 'words of knowledge' – you are not claiming inspired discernment. It is a method by which the truth about Christ can come alive for you, take on depth and colour. In the light of the image you may see the features of Christ.

For example, I remember being part of a group concentrating in this way on a few verses from Ephesians (3:14–21). One man was drawn to the image of being filled with the fullness of Christ and fleshed out the picture with memories of digging holes in the sand when he was a child at the beach. However big the hole he dug it was not large enough to drain the ocean. In fact, the tide came in effortlessly and filled the hole. The larger the hole the more water poured into it. For him it became a picture of prayer as digging a hole for God to fill and intercessory prayer as digging on behalf of others. Another member of the group, looking at the same passage, was taken by the image of Christ dwelling in us – coming to live permanently rather than being restricted by our lukewarm welcome to pop in just as a day visitor. Another person filled out the picture of God's glorious riches with an image of God with a large sack overflowing with presents, scattering them around with reckless generosity. 'Rooted in love' gave rise to the image of a tree growing tall, buffeted by the wind but not blown over, stretching its branches towards heaven and becoming a shelter for birds.

I must stress that such pictures are not claims to divine inspiration. And, of course, at their most banal, they can be versions of 'Life's like a sardine tin'. Nevertheless playing with an image can release facets of a biblical metaphor that the intellect, in its busyness, can fail to reach and by so doing, can touch depths in us and our relationship with Christ.

LETTING THE PICTURE MOVE

A third method, used for hundreds of years, visualizes scenes from the gospels. Here the imagination is fully engaged in picturing the scene. It is often helpful to say to yourself as you live in, say, the story of Mary and Martha in Luke 10:38–42, 'What am I seeing? Hearing? Smelling? Touching? Tasting?' The scene begins to come alive in three dimensions with colour and sound. Visualize the event as vividly as you can.

It may be difficult to describe what happens next but continue to look at the scene until 'the picture begins to move'. You may wish just to watch the characters, listening to them speak and observing their interaction. As an alternative you can become one of the characters and speak to Jesus or hear him speaking to you. You may wish to be yourself and enter the scene, engaging with the other participants.

In my experience time spent living in the story, chewing over scripture, allowing the imagination to work on the scene, using all the senses, is never wasted. At times it can be the source of encounters with Christ of a profound and even life-changing kind. I have already mentioned in Chapter 3 the experience of a man who employed this method in relation to the wedding at Cana.

One cannot predict what effect a story will have. I remember speaking to a man who had meditated on the story of Easter day. In his imagination he was sitting in the tomb, hunched up, as he recalls, on one of the stone slabs, looking at the grave clothes. To his left, he was aware of steps going up to the entrance, though he was unable to see outside. The tomb was dark, lit only by one guttering candle, but from the opening the morning sunlight poured in. Suddenly he was aware of the voice of Christ saying, 'What are you doing here, hiding in the dark, looking at a candle when outside the world is bathed in sunlight? I am not in here. I am outside.' For him the words spoke not just of Easter but were directly relevant to the way he was living his life.

The gospels are full of such pictures; they come to us as still lifes but they are waiting to move and through them Christ will meet us again and again. Often the best advice is not to turn the page until the picture comes alive for you. At the end of Luke's gospel there is a freeze-frame of Jesus that never ceases to stir me (Luke 24:40–43). It catches a simple action, mundane, earthly, grossly materialistic, almost banal. The disciples in the upper room think Jesus is a ghost and he asks them, 'Have you got anything to eat?' Where have you heard that before? It's the cry of the ravenous teenage son: 'What's in the fridge?' The disciples say, 'We've just had supper but there's a bit of broiled fish.' And he eats it in front of them.

And here I am confronted with a Jesus who is real, in my kitchen, as it were. There he stands, just to the right as you stand at the sink, leaning against the Savannah working surface, next to the toaster. It's a Jesus who walks into my living room asking, 'What CDs have you got?' A Jesus seated at the dinner table, laughing, and saying, 'The *crème brûlée* is fantastic.' Or sitting in the passenger seat of the car saying, 'Are you worried about this appointment?' Or walking with me as I go to a difficult meeting and reassuring me with the words 'I've been here before you and prepared the way.'

OUR SEEING RINSED AND CLEANSED

There are many resources available for those who want to take this theme further and find out more about praying into and through the scriptures. However, at the risk of repetition, nothing is more important than the desire to see the face of Christ through our reading. Augustine said, 'Longing is the heart's treasury.' To become like Christ is what Christianity is all about. To be like him is the key to our true humanity. To see his face is to live with our 'seeing rinsed'. From that point

onwards the world carries the memory that once it was trans-
figured and holds the promise that one day it will be so again.
All this may seem a long way from the FTSE and the price
of petrol but it is the goal of the life of faith. As so often
Augustine, this time preaching on 'the light of your face' from
Psalm 44:3, says it all: Christ is

> lovely in heaven, lovely upon earth, lovely in the womb,
> lovely in his parents' arms, lovely in his works of
> power, lovely under the scourge's blow, lovely in bidding
> men live, lovely in scorn of death, lovely yielding up his
> life, lovely taking it again, lovely on the Tree, lovely in
> the tomb, lovely at last in heaven.

REFLECTION

Try the three methods of reading the scriptures outlined
above. For *lectio divina* perhaps choose one of the Psalms
(Psalm 121 or 126 might be good ones). Give yourself half an
hour of uninterrupted time. Follow the pattern of read, meditate (ruminate), pray and contemplate.

For *playing with images* try any passage in the epistles.
They are full of pictures in words waiting to be unpacked.

For *letting the picture move* an incident from the gospels
may be best. Luke 10:38–42; 19:1–10; Matthew 21:1–11 are
possible ones.

For all three methods you will move at some point into
stage three of the *lectio divina* process – praying. If your
reading has stirred a response in your heart, talk it over with
God. What feelings have bubbled to the surface: joy, guilt,
tiredness, love, anger, awe? Whatever they are, share them
with your heavenly Father, knowing that he receives you as
you are.

The final stage may be the hardest part. Put your Bible
down, sit silently, clear your mind and wait. You may find it
helpful to concentrate on the rhythm of your own breathing,

and sit with your hands held palms-upwards. Don't try to do anything; just rest in God's company. If illuminating ideas or pictures come to you, thank God for them but don't hang on to them; return simply to being with him and letting him make the running. When the moment is right, give thanks and return to the business of the day.

DISCUSSION

'Transfigurations cannot be timetabled.' Have you had 'mountain-top experiences' that you can share? In what ways did these experiences come unbidden? Were they followed by failures?

'Moments of glory may come unbidden but they do not have to be unlooked for. It is our responsibility to be awake to the possibility. This entails watching out for the Master, keeping vigil with him in regular prayer and meditation, and taking advantage of times out of the routine of daily life.' How do you 'keep vigil'? What gets in the way of taking time out?

PRAYER

> Lord Jesus Christ,
> Living word,
> Meet me in the pages of this book.
>
> Break the bread and feed my soul.
> Split the rock and quench my thirst.
>
> Touch my heart with the flame of your love.
> Lighten my path with the lamp of your truth.
> Still my spirit with the beauty of your peace
>
> And let me see you face to face.

Epilogue

Everyone agrees that Jesus is elusive. The titles of books suggest it: *The Jesus They Never Told You About, The Man Nobody Knows*. Albert Schweitzer ended his quest of the historical Jesus with the words 'He comes to us as one unknown'. Ezra Pound put into the mouth of Simon the Zealot the words 'They'll no get him a' in a book I think'. In John 6 the crowds pursue Jesus across the lake and, at the end of the feeding miracle, try by force to make him king. But he slips away, ever the elusive Jesus, in no one's pocket, always demonstrating the freedom of God.

At the end of this book I am more conscious than ever that Jesus will not be pigeon-holed or controlled. I am less concerned about what I have made of him, than what he makes of me. The icon of the Christ Pantocrator, Christ the ruler of all, stares at me disturbingly out of the frame. But then so do all the icons of Jesus as an infant. Usually gaunt and austere, occasionally chubby and well fed, the child contemplates me with a serene gaze, appraising me, taking all I am into account. I once heard a specialist on icons say, 'People buy copies of icons to hang on the walls of their sitting rooms. They think icons are there for them to look at. They don't realize that you don't look at an icon; it looks at you.'

The book has contained relatively little about the Jesus of judgement – the Christ with the whip of cords, storming through the temple courts, overturning tables and setting pigeons free. We are always to quick to patronize him. The words of the carol address him as 'darling, darling, little man'. But the gospels record on more than one occasion that there was a *schisma*, a division, a rending or tear, because of him. He divided people, provoked hostility, precipitated a crisis.

In T. S. Eliot's phrase, Jesus comes as 'the one who knows how to ask questions'. He seldom asks for information and his questions go to the heart of the matter. 'Do you want to be healed?' he asks someone who has been ill for thirty-eight years (John 5:6). Isn't the answer obvious? But Jesus knows perhaps that hope has died and needs to be revived. 'Woman, what have I to do with you?' is a harsh question to his mother. But she, of all people, knows that trying to control and manipulate her son is not the way to serve him best. 'Is it right to do good on the Sabbath or to do evil?', 'Which of these was neighbour to him who fell among thieves?', 'Where shall we buy bread that these may eat?' are all deceptively simple and obvious questions. And they all expose the real issue, the real struggle, the place of resistance – and possible healing. This is the hard edge of loving.

It was Bishop David Jenkins who said that, in his experience, Christ was the great disturber. His values turn ours upside down. He goes to the centre of religious activity and attacks the establishment in the name of God. He condemns those who make much of religious observance, tithing garden herbs and yet neglecting mercy and justice. He looks around with anger at those who are unwilling to recognize the challenge of the truth because it conflicts with their rigid system. He censures those who twist and turn in order to deny what their hearts tell them. The unforgivable sin is to see the truth and then turn away from it deliberately. This is the sin against the Spirit.

He makes unreasonable demands, the kind that only God has the right to make. 'Sell all you have and follow me', 'no one putting his hand to the plough and looking back is fit for the kingdom of God', 'enter by the narrow gate'. We hold family dear to us. We expect to be commanded to love our families and so we are – in a sense. But the teaching on family ties is marked more by its radical undercutting of the family than by its support for Victorian family values: 'I have come to turn a man against his father, a daughter against her mother, a daughter-in-law against her mother-in-law – a man's enemies will be the members of his own household' (Matthew 10:34ff.). Marriage and the family are one of life's most important commitments, but the loyalty to God is overriding. In the end a man or a woman must leave all in order to follow Christ; discipleship changes everything and revises all allegiances.

We see money as a blessing and assume that if you have it, you are fortunate. The big issue then is about being generous with what you've got. Jesus' view on money is consistent, radical – and utterly scandalous. He seems to treat it like a plague. If you have money then you are in terrible danger. It's like poison. Hold on to it and it will kill you. Delight in riches will spread its tentacles around your heart. Get it off your hands as fast as possible. Camels can go through needles' eyes quicker. How hard it is for a rich man to enter the kingdom of heaven.

We can understand how Francis Thompson could depict Christ as the hound of heaven and why C. S. Lewis chose a lion, Aslan – but not a tame lion – to be the Christ figure in the Narnia chronicles. He interrogates my devious heart, condemns my pious evasions of responsibility and disrupts my comfortable lifestyle. He is a stone of stumbling and a rock of offence. How can I speak of the attractiveness of Jesus?

It may seem a paradox but it is in the uncompromising stance of Jesus towards us that we may see a new facet of his attractiveness. We expect God to be nice, to care for us and make us feel good. In Jesus we encounter real love, love like steel, love that makes your eyes water like a cold wind on a frosty day. To quote a friend's way of putting it, 'Jesus cuts the crap.' He tells it like it is, will not be diverted from the truth, will not duck the hard question or be fobbed off with claptrap. Such honest love is exhilarating, and is such a rare experience. We can rely on him to tell us exactly how it is.

But along with that fidelity to the truth of the matter goes a fierce commitment to our good. We all have friends who tell us home truths from time to time. Sometimes we suspect they are getting a grudge off their chest in the guise of concern for our welfare. But Jesus really is for us. When he speaks the truth to us, we know that he is wholly on our side. In him we meet someone who is obsessed with our welfare, who will not give up on the project come what may, who is more committed to us than we are to ourselves. That doesn't happen to us very often.

His commitment to us entails deep respect for our freedom. In the gospels Jesus shows how much he values people in the way he receives them. He gives everyone dignity and worth. Even Judas is respected. Jesus' words 'What you are about to do, do quickly' (John 13:27) honour the decision of the one who is about to betray him and thus give him the dignity of a responsible agent. Christ takes our responses to him with immense seriousness. At the end he accepts and ratifies the choices we make about him. But to be treated as someone accountable, as someone who makes free and responsible choices is one of the biggest compliments anyone can pay us.

I have tried to suggest that Jesus is never in our pockets. He retains the freedom to challenge our conventions, to scandalize our assumptions and to trespass on our comfort zones. If I try to contain him he will lead me a merry dance. I don't often come across a refiner's fire and the thought that the flames are to purify me and make me all I was designed to be is both terrifying and strangely heartening.

And suddenly, just to show that if you set off after the divine fox you will not run him to ground, I come across a passage in the gospels that leaves me gasping for breath:

> Jesus knew that the Father had put all things under his power, and that he had come from God and was returning to God; so he got up from the meal, took off his outer clothing, and wrapped a towel round his waist. After that, he poured water into a basin and began to wash his disciples' feet, drying them with the towel that was wrapped round him. (John 13:3–5)

Deity on its knees.
'They'll no get him a' in a book I think.'
But you already knew that.

ACKNOWLEDGEMENTS

Extract from 'A Touching Place' from *Love from Below* (Wild Goose Publications, 1989) by John L. Bell and Graham Maule. Copyright © 1989 WGRG, The Iona Community, 840 Govan Road, Glasgow G51 3UU, Scotland.

Extract from *Love for the Lost* (Penguin, 2000) by Catherine Fox. Reproduced by kind permission of the author.

Extract from 'The Transfiguration' from *Collected Poems* (Faber and Faber, 1960) by Edwin Muir. Reproduced by permission of Faber and Faber, London.

Extract from 'In a country church' from *Collected Poems 1945–1990* (J. M. Dent, 1995) by R. S. Thomas. Reproduced by permission of The Orion Publishing Group, London.